Lionel Trilling

Lionel Trilling

CRITICISM AND POLITICS

William M. Chace

STANFORD UNIVERSITY PRESS

Stanford, California   1980

The photograph of Lionel Trilling on the
previous page is from the files of *The Colum-
bian* and appears with the permission of the
Board of Editors.

Stanford University Press
Stanford, California

© 1980 by the Board of Trustees of the
Leland Stanford Junior University

Printed in the United States of America
ISBN 0-8047-1032-5
LC 78-66173

To the memory of my father
WILLIAM EMERSON CHACE, 1902–1975
who worked hard, had patience
and loved his family

Acknowledgments

COLLEAGUES AT STANFORD and elsewhere have helped me write this book. They have been generous and I wish formally to thank them here: Herbert Lindenberger, Donald Davie, Ian Watt, Thomas Flanagan, John Henry Raleigh, and Frederick Crews. I owe enormous gratitude for the incisive and imaginative suggestions given me by Mark Shechner of the State University of New York at Buffalo. Joseph Epstein of *The American Scholar* provided welcome encouragement. Three students at Stanford, John Vargas, Michael Perez, and Kenneth Whiting, gave me important assistance when I needed it. Lawrence Rothfield, a student at Columbia University, and Richard Yankwich, Esq. assisted me in technical matters. My wife, JoAn, was intelligent about everything. Our two children rightly saw at times that I required help.

Contents

Preface

THIS STUDY is of Trilling's important writings, not of his life. Doubtless there are personal aspects of his literary and political involvements that might prove interesting to many a reader, but they are not examined here. That substantial part of Trilling's achievement which history will find memorable, that "best" and deepest self, exists, I am convinced, in his published prose, not elsewhere. Upon his death, his friend and fellow-teacher at Columbia, Jacques Barzun, found it appropriate to say of him, rephrasing Stendhal's epitaph: "He lived, he taught, he wrote."[1] Barzun meant to suggest, I believe, that his colleague had led a private, not a public life. I agree, adding only that Trilling's special intellectual privacies were in time to become a public possession. A proper consideration of his career will show, moreover, that far from being simply one of and like many in the literary and intellectual circles of New York City, he was alone in the depth and capacity of his critical vision. That singularity made of him a very powerful critical presence.

I write this book on Trilling from California, and not from New York. As someone born exactly one year before the German invasion of Poland, I do not know at firsthand many aspects of the modern experience of ideological conflict. Stalin is to me a name, not an experience. I am not Jewish. For these reasons, and for others, I am separated to some degree from the milieu—historical, political, and social—that was Trilling's. I am consoled, however, by the recognition that every writer on a literary or critical figure suffers from some such separation. None of us ever becomes wholly "at one" with our subjects. The value of our work in fact consists in what we are able to do with the disadvantage at which we are placed—by history, by political and social developments, by the changes in perspective that the movement of generations inevitably brings.

W.M.C.

Lionel Trilling

1. Introduction

OF LIONEL TRILLING, upon his death in November 1975, *The New York Times* said: "He made the life of the mind an exciting experience. Yet, as a critic he founded no school and left no group of disciples closely associated with his name." As one much absorbed in the study of how truth resides in, and is left out of, statements of simple fact, Trilling himself might have found much to ponder in so simple an obituary statement. For the statement is true enough, yet oddly false. He founded no school; his thought has no system from which one can easily borrow either parts or techniques; and his disciples were errant, becoming in time as disparate as any teachers' students can become. Allen Ginsberg, John Hollander, Norman Podhoretz, and Steven Marcus, all once students at Columbia, were mentioned in the *Times* obituary. They constitute no group.

Yet surely a critic without a system or without numerous well-known active disciples can be a figure of extraordinary influence. Lionel Trilling was such a critic. His students were so many, in fact, that their names matter less than their number. And his thought, which at once overrode and abjured systems, has been more decisively influential in the culture of which it is now a permanent part than systems customarily are.

Irving Howe, a critic of a later generation deeply affected by Trilling, wrote of him upon his death that he had "believed passionately—and taught a whole generation also to believe—in the power of literature, its power to transform, elevate and damage." [1] One might go a step beyond Howe and

say that Trilling, more successfully than any other literary
critic of his time and of his place—mid-century America—
made his own generation of intellectuals reconsider. That
generation was asked to reconsider some of its deepest working assumptions, to reflect upon its literary, political, and
moral beliefs. Literature was to be seen, as Matthew Arnold
had once seen it, as the best judge of life; politics was to be
seen under the shadow of Stalinism; morality could not be
seen at all unless seen as infinitely complex. And in time that
generation did learn to reconsider, and with profit to its sense
of itself. Trilling had been its moral teacher; he had shown
ways in which the imaginative power of literature could
probe the process of individual moral development.

It was the sense of self, or the tension held perpetually
among the several aspects of self, that preoccupied Trilling in
his writings. That preoccupation began in the 1920's, in the
pages of *The Menorah Journal*, and was patiently sustained,
decade after decade, essay after essay, down to his posthu-
mously published remarks on "Why We Read Jane Austen."
Out of his own diplomacy (never a war) with himself, he
made his criticism. Thus, over the years Trilling always drew
on his sense of self in order to interpret the society surrounding him. That society changed greatly in the exact half-
century (1925 to 1975) in which he wrote. In the 1930's it
was subject to political stresses so powerful that the generation
of American intellectuals of which Trilling was a member
was still recoiling from the effects four decades later. The
siren-song of radical political involvement, and the painful
entanglements of Stalinism, could still be heard and felt by
that generation. Just as his society underwent transformations, however, so did he. Thus, though the process of his
critical interpretation went on without a stop, the fundamental terms of the process—individual self within and collective
selves without—were always subject to alteration.

As a literary critic, he knew what his times had impressed
upon him: that the relationships between important forces in

any culture are dynamic; that nothing significant can remain imprisoned in the definition once given to it; and that things become themselves by resolving, without perfect success, their latent oppositions. Behind Trilling in this conviction stood those thinkers to whom he constantly returned over the years: Freud, Hegel, and Marx. He confronted each with ambivalence. Freud held his greatest allegiance and respect. Hegel was an authority with whom he always had to reckon; his teachings about life consisted of ironies stressed so powerfully that they became the highest wisdom. Marx was a serious danger and a significant challenge; his nineteenth-century researches, pursued with enormous cerebral strength, had become twentieth-century murders, conducted with nightmarish obsessiveness. But each of these three had become, for Trilling, a representation of the truth that complex mutabilities dominated his time.

Part of this understanding was his recognition that literature is not a passive representation of forces superior in consequence to itself. It is not a product, a "yield." In becoming consequential within a society, moreover, it can come to oppose the very circumstances that have seen it rise into being. What Trilling termed the "adversary culture" was an intense example of culture, in its mutability, engendering a literature antagonistic to itself. He believed that the spirit of alienation and disenchantment characteristic of literary modernism was a profound example of culture working against its own premises. When he speaks, then, of that "adversary culture," and when he points to the "actually subversive intention, that characterizes modern writing,"[2] he is acknowledging the idea that culture, in becoming divided against itself, can be imperious and threatening. Literature is no object; literature is not benign. And no literary critic can function well if he believes his duty is to domesticate literature.

In considering, in 1961, the sorts of writing that had "fallen" to him to teach at Columbia College, he was to say that "almost all of them have been involved with me for a long

time—I invert the natural order not out of lack of modesty
but taking the cue of W. H. Auden's remark that a real book
reads us. . . . Some of these books at first rejected me; I bored
them. But as I grew older and they knew me better, they
came to have more sympathy with me and to understand my
hidden meanings."[3]

A "real" book reads *us*. A culture, particularly modern culture, does not come into being until after it has been felt as
an imposition. Born of antagonism, it exists as the record of
how such antagonism, between self and created artistic object,
has moved toward resolution. Trilling was to confess anxieties in the face of the impositions he saw everywhere around
him as manifestations of modern culture. He was at times to
feel cowed by them. He knew at last that he did not really *like*
much of modern literature.* He did not, however, succumb
to the anxieties he felt. He recognized that the very oppositions, challenges, and impositions that it had been his career
to study were a large part of his own self. Hence he had to
determine as fully as he could how self might exist amid oppositions. Thus the lesson of Hegel.

About Hegel Trilling was to write much, some of it in
oblique tribute and some of it, particularly in *Sincerity and
Authenticity* (his last book, 1972), in objective analysis. It
was Hegel, Trilling wrote in 1955, "who first spoke of the
'alienation' which the modern self contrives as a means for
the fulfillment of its destiny, and of the pain which the self
incurs because of this device of self-realization."[4] Alienation
from one's culture is inevitable and painful; but it is also,
ironically, the very process by which the self resolves its own
contradictions and pushes toward fulfillment. This "strange,

* Writing in the last year of his life, he gave succinct expression to the
densely entangled feelings he had had toward the high artistic culture of
the modern age: "Before most of it I stood puzzled, abashed and a little
queasy; I was at least as much alienated from it as I was from the culture to
which it opposed itself." "A Personal Memoir," in *From Parnassus: Essays
in Honor of Jacques Barzun,* ed. Dora B. Weiner and William R. Keylor
(New York, 1976), p. xxi.

bitter, dramatic" process is at the very center of personal existence made social. It is what becoming "cultured" in a serious and not merely fashionable sense happens to be. As a
process, it encouraged Trilling to become a *public* critic of
literature and society, to make his mind not his alone but re-
flective of the social life surrounding it, a social life whose
meaningful existence was not really to be questioned, whose
substantiality was never in doubt. To understand Trilling is
to appreciate how, over a long career, that process of becoming—and always failing to become—wholly cultured, wholly
social, and resolutely public was his central drama. The drama
disclosed itself slowly, and with the kind of stately circumspection for which, in time, Trilling as a prose stylist became well
known.

He once said "I have a weakness for the general subject."[5]
That general subject, the personal self in perpetual but generative unease with its culture, was his teaching. Hence Trilling may most profitably be considered in terms not of his
disciples or his system but of the representative mind he
sought to possess. He patiently taught minds like his own, of
a time like his own, to see that his long and enormously attentive engagement with his surroundings might very well be
their engagement with similar surroundings. In that sense Arnoldian, he offered his own capacious reflections on the self's
"bitter" struggles so that he might clarify the thinking of each
of his readers. The late poet and short-story writer Delmore
Schwartz, unhappy with Trilling but nonetheless enlivened
by him, wrote in 1953 that "Mr. Trilling is interested in the
ideas and attitudes and interests of the educated class, such as
it is and such as it may become: it is of this class that he is, at
heart, the guardian and the critic."[6] This was meant as censorious, but it is accurate while also being reductive. Trilling
did interest himself in, and at last represented, a certain class.
He became its loyal guardian and its solicitous critic. This
class of which Schwartz speaks is not, however, small. It possesses much of the power that conscious culture in our society

has. It includes, among many others, the readers of this book. It once embraced Schwartz. It is no little province. It is occupied by teachers and scientists, intellectuals and artists; its borders are vague but broad. By other descriptions it could be called "the life of the mind." To that life Trilling, for some fifty years, brought the attention of his contradictory and discerning intelligence.

2. History and Response

THE WAYS IN WHICH an intellectual holds his past in mind can be at once revealing and deceptive. In any writer's hands the "past" becomes a chronicle whose inclusions and omissions are not accidental. The story one wants to tell becomes the story one had to tell. Along the way, some parts of the past are neglected.

For a good part of his life Lionel Trilling was particularly interested in one story, and his peculiar telling of it reveals now, to us, important qualities of his mind. The story was that of "the radical thirties," the political temptations of the time, and the lessons learned in a period of intense engagement and its long aftermath. He looked back to the Depression decade as indispensable to his intellectual development, but he never looked back to it without misgivings. The past taught hard lessons. It had been a dramatic time, but it had left, as he said in 1966, "a sour taste in the mouths of many." To him, and to others, it "had brought to the fore a peculiarly American desiccation of temperament."[1]

With a past so strong and yet so repugnant, one response available to Trilling would have been to have conferred upon it a look less ravaged and painful. Trilling seems to have recognized this danger, and to have avoided it. In the 1960's, he knew that no glory was alive in the Depression period. The 1930's were not a chapter of history suitable to sentimental or elegiac treatment. They were history conditioned by large economic and political pressures. Beneath those pressures, people had changed and adapted to new demands. In the long

wake of those changes, intellectual life in New York City and
elsewhere in the country was given its particular direction. In
1966, he went over the history in commenting on an almost
forgotten novel of the earlier time, Tess Slesinger's *The Un-
possessed* (published in 1934):

> In any view of the American cultural situation, the importance
> of the radical movement of the Thirties cannot be overestimated.
> It may be said to have created the American intellectual class as
> we now know it in its great size and influence. It fixed the charac-
> ter of this class as being, through all mutations of opinion, pre-
> dominantly of the Left. And quite apart from opinion, the politi-
> cal tendency of the Thirties defined the style of the class—from
> that radicalism came the moral urgency, the sense of crisis, and
> the concern with personal salvation that mark the existence of
> American intellectuals.[2]

The judgment here is a historical one. So too is his remark,
in the same essay, that the class of intellectuals of which he
speaks (and for whom, in many ways, he wound up speaking)
had departed from radical politics "with despair."[3]

Trilling's perception of the journey taken by his class is not
peculiar to him. It has been charted by many people, some
of them his contemporaries, some not. All agree that most of
the American intellectuals of Trilling's background passed
through the intensities of Depression radicalism; were drawn
to one or another of the temptations of the Left; recoiled
after the Communist-Socialist and Stalinist-Trotskyist feuds of
the late 1930's; came to the shocks of recognition posed by
war in Spain, trials in the Soviet Union, and the Nazi-Soviet
pact; and then pursued more than two decades of *rapprochement* with the values of the American bourgeoisie to which
they had for so long been hostile. The surviving participants
are now busily writing up the last chapters of this story.

Trilling's own historical coverage of this arc of transit is
briefer and much vaguer than that of many others who were
involved. Neither in the essay just mentioned nor in any other
place does he describe that long arc in any greater substance
or detail. Comparison of his account with some others is en-

lightening. For instance, Dwight Macdonald's treatment of his own "Politics Past," written in 1957, has about it a fascination with the peculiar circumstances and small hard facts that went to make up his time and place. Macdonald says, as does Trilling, that his career has described an arc or parabola, but he goes on to provide a specificity not attempted by Trilling:

In the late thirties the *avant-garde* political spectrum looked like this, reading from left to right: *Communists* (who had moved overnight, on orders from Moscow, from the far left to the extreme right, becoming "critical supporters" of the New Deal and later not-at-all critical supporters of the war), *Social Democrats* (a small but well-heeled group of aging right-wing Socialists centering around the Rand School and the weekly *New Leader*), *Socialists* (led by Eugene Debs in World War One and now by Norman Thomas), *"Lovestoneites"* . . . , *Socialist Workers Party* (Trotskyites, led by James P. Cannon and Max Shachtman, former Communists who had founded the party when Trotsky was exiled by Stalin in 1929 and who still lead it—or rather each leads one of the halves into which it split in 1940), *Socialist Labor Party.* . . .[4]

Macdonald's history goes on to cite other factions, other splinter groups; it lingers over the schisms and tempests then so momentous and now, to him, so absurd. Histories such as his are written on the understanding that they must be lengthy and involved if they are to capture the gritty substance out of which political reality slowly forms. Trilling's account, by contrast, includes little such substance. It stands above discussions of schisms and factions; to him, the Left in that past time was apparently a monolith. Nor does his account reflect another important aspect of that history, one to which other commentators have sharply drawn attention. In describing the *embourgeoisement* of the American intelligentsia during the 1950's, Irving Howe has commented:

The world seemed to be opening up, with all its charms, seductions, and falsities. In the 30's the life of the New York writers had been confined: the little magazine as island, the radical sect as cave. Partly they were recapitulating the pattern of immigrant

Jewish experience: an ingathering of the flock in order to break out into the world and taste the Gentile fruits of status and success.[5]

What is explicit here is never explicit in Trilling: the transit Howe undertook, and Trilling undertook, and the one undertaken by many others, was a particular experience, largely Jewish in nature. It involved patterns of Jewish assimilation; New York City was its center. And Lionel Trilling, a native New Yorker, a life-long resident of Manhattan, and for some forty years a teacher at Columbia University, was involved in that assimilation. Such history and such sociology are hardly esoteric areas of knowledge, but they figure nowhere in Trilling's form of history. He writes as one for whom the fact of his own Jewishness figures only as a reality *against* which he defines himself, never *within* which he finds his definition. Jewishness apparently had to be transcended if it were to take on any significance at all to him. Thus as early as 1944 he wrote, in response to questions about Jewish cultural identity posed by the *Contemporary Jewish Record*: "I do not think of myself as a 'Jewish writer.' I do not have it in mind to serve by my writing any Jewish purpose. I should resent it if a critic of my work were to discover in it either faults or virtues which he called Jewish." * Indeed, the only aspect of Jewishness important to Trilling in 1944 was that it made possible the saving grace of alienation: "the great fact for American Jews is their exclusion from certain parts of the general life and every activity of Jewish life seems to be a re-

*See Trilling's contribution to "Under Forty: A Symposium on American Literature and the Younger Generation of American Jews," *Contemporary Jewish Record*, vii, no. 1 (Feb. 1944), p. 15. These feelings were renewed in 1962, in his "Introduction" to Robert Warshow's *The Immediate Experience: Movies, Comics, Theatre, and Other Aspects of Popular Culture* (New York, 1962), when he reported that he had once declined to serve on the advisory committee for *Commentary* magazine: "I had had my experience of the intellectual life lived in reference to . . . the Jewish community, and I had no wish to renew it by associating myself with a Jewish magazine." He went on to say that the impulses of Warshow's work "came from sources that were anything but Jewish." *The Immediate Experience*, p. 14.

sponse to this fact."[6] Two decades later, in the essay on Tess
Slesinger's novel, this observation is made again, but now to
demonstrate that the only significance of anti-Semitism is that
it, too, can and must be transcended. Speaking of the Jews of
his own intellectual generation, he says: "If the anti-Semitism
that we observed did not arouse our indignation, this was in
part because we took it to be a kind of advantage: against this
social antagonism we could define ourselves *and* our society,
we could discover who we were and who we wished to be. It
helped to give life the look of reality."[7]

Being a Jew and being a victim of anti-Jewish feeling
amount, for Trilling, to the same thing. Both are states of
being thrust upon an individual by society. But that individual need not remain passive in the face of them. He can turn
aside their force and then occupy a station superior to them.
In this way, he acquires a "reality" or a "look of reality" useful
to him for other purposes. One's Jewishness seen either as fortune or tribulation is not as important as one's Jewishness
seen as a way into, and out of, society. Hence the discovery of
his own Jewish situation made "society at last available to my
imagination," or so Trilling reported.[8] But it also apparently
made history and society—so consequential in their specific
density to other intellectuals of Trilling's time or slightly
later, to people like Macdonald or Howe—somehow secondary to Trilling himself. Things of specific density fell away
from his mind just as brute matter fell away from the minds of
the symbolist poets who transmuted the everyday into the im-
perishable. Society and history are thus rendered in his vision
ancillary to what he saw as a more serious and exalted pursuit.
That pursuit was his literary criticism. Its high-flown nature
owes much to his transcendence of certain forms of local identity and local circumstance. In sum, the history in which Trilling was so decisively uninterested takes social circumstances
as the pattern of *final* understanding. He looked on those circumstances merely as a point of departure. Where another
critic might see history as a determinant, he saw it as no more

than a setting against which a real event—an event of the mind and the critical imagination—takes place.

Trilling's transcendent manner may be contrasted also to a "traditional" or normative description of the political history through which he and others passed. The description comes from the Trotskyist George Novack and is part of his eulogy in *The Militant* for Herbert Solow, born two years before Trilling (in 1903), a close friend of Trilling's as a Columbia undergraduate, and, like Trilling, an early contributor to *The Menorah Journal*:

Herbert was a most representative figure of his generation. His itinerary mirrored that of a constellation of American intellectuals who were impelled to the left by the 1929 depression, swung into the orbit of the Communist Party, became disillusioned with Stalinism and broke sharply with it, collaborated in varying degrees for different lengths of time with the Trotskyist movement and then with the onset of the Second World War or shortly thereafter turned entirely away from radicalism.[9]

To this eulogy, and to the standard, or received, historical perspective it represents, Trilling would have taken no exception. But it is the very sort of description and classification in which his interest was not grounded. Trotsky, for instance, was really present in history, yet he makes no entry in Trilling's history. Also present in history was the Second World War, but the war figures only distantly and cloudily in Trilling's writing. The Depression, the Communist Party, the chaotic turbulence of radicalism—they exert a strong but somehow quite vague force in his critical prose. And so, referring to Daniel Aaron's *Writers on the Left*, generally regarded as the most informative survey of American intellectuals during the 1930's, Trilling commented that "a reading of this useful work might lead to the conclusion that no politics was ever drearier."[10] The "dreariness" of this politics, and of politics in general, made Trilling react in a peculiar way to it. He was oblivious to its sharp, intense specifics, but utterly alive to its large, symbolic importance. One feels always in reading Trilling that the political history to which he was responsive was one that had become abstract, coagulated and general. It was history as Moral Lesson—not history as local and immediate imperative. He responded not to events, but to the past as it had become encrusted with ethical meaning. Impatient with detail, tragic in his reading of the larger consequences, and aspiring to be patriarchal in his wisdom, Trilling was always involved in what he saw as the moral reality of his surroundings. In the decades after the 1930's, as historical and political detail constantly lost weight in his evaluations, and as Significance constantly gained it, he rode above the narrow constraints supplied by the traditional historians and was absorbed by the paradigms that can be developed only by the enlarged moral mind.*

Knowing these things, one knows better how to read Trilling. One knows what to look for, and what never to expect. He was not, nor did he think of himself as, a register of events; to consider him as such is to miss sight of him entirely and to ignore his real critical power. His criticism grew out of his ingenious negotiation of the passage leading directly away from the immediacy of radical politics. Over a career of many years, that passage led toward an acceptance of the complex moral drama of possessing, if little power to change circumstances, then much liberty to analyze them, some grounds on which to base a sober affection for the United States, and an understanding of the appropriateness of employing "moral

---

*Mark Shechner puts it this way: "Such sensitivity to ideology and its effects, based as it was upon a belief in the primacy of thought, was bought at a price; here, as elsewhere, Trilling suppressed those dimensions of social reality that progressive realism played up: the depression, the unemployment, the vicious labor battles, the advances of Fascism in Europe—in short, the general desperation." (Mark Shechner, "Psychoanalysis and Liberalism: The Case of Lionel Trilling," *Salmagundi*, no. 41 [Spring 1978], p. 12.) Where Shechner sees Trilling's energies channeled into "suppression," I see them given over to transcendence. Shechner's explanation and his diction are more resolutely psychological than are mine.

realism" and "irony" to grasp contemporary conditions. This passage was, in sum, the long one from the 1930's to the 1950's and 1960's.

Reflecting on the generation of New York intellectuals who followed that passage, Howe has commented that their sensibility was one of "rootless radicalism," and a radicalism, moreover, "beginning to decay at the very moment it was adopted."[11] Surely Howe is correct about this: the exposure of American intellectuals to Marxist ideas was intensive for only a short time, from October 1929 to the creation of the mollifying "Popular Front" campaigns in the country and elsewhere in 1935–36 and thereafter. After those fiery few years, radicalism was seen by intellectuals either as less ideologically compelling and therefore more acceptable (the United States and the USSR became allies of a sort, after all, against the common enemy of fascism), or as more morally suspect and therefore less acceptable (in the USSR Stalin's purges spread, liquidating "enemies," real or imagined, Trotskyist and otherwise). The upshot of these complex changes was that if true Communist radicalism had once been a fire in the United States, it was soon isolated and its spread halted after a few short years. If it had been a beacon of hope, it flared up only to flicker out quickly. The intellectuals involved in this intense historical moment had, Howe says, come late: *after* the real immigrant Jewish experience (the quota system was in full force after 1924). Moreover, what radicalism they had come to possess in so short a time was soon choked off when, after 1941, a country more or less united went to war. This spasmodic involvement in radicalism, and its remarkably long and consequential aftermath, were described in 1962 by another of those involved in both, the editor and essayist William Phillips:

After a time it was just assumed that the verdict of history was in —against socialism. And, as we can now see, the anti-Communist mood merged with a growing acceptance of the life of this country, and of the West, as a whole. Content does not usually stimu-

late radical feelings; and any discontent that could not be repressed was diffused into concern with the human condition, as
in existentialism, or transformed into sexual revolt, which has
become the rebellious mode of our time. Socialism—indeed any
form of radicalism—was assumed to be a doctrine for those romantics who were either too young to remember the past or too
old to forget it.[12]

Howe tells us that Trilling was from an aftermath generation, Phillips that that generation took its leave from socialism
and moved toward personal contentment and self-regard.
From either perspective, the implications for a proper understanding of Trilling are the same: he reacted to the claims of
the past with a refusal to permit any one thing—be it his own
Jewishness, his own memories of leftist temptation, or his own
devotion to the classic texts of literary modernism—to determine his identity. The past had no greater effect on him than
to spur him to resist being its mere consequence.

The historian David A. Hollinger has supplied a general
understanding of the situation after the 1930's that may be
applied effectively to Trilling's individual situation. Hollinger describes Jewish "cosmopolitanism" and the way it developed:

The intelligentsia that came fully into its own in the 1940s was
formed primarily by the merger of two, originally autonomous
revolts against two distinctive provincialisms, and what mattered
most about the Jewish immigrants was not their ethnicity, nor
even their inherited devotion to learning, but their impatience
with the limitations of ethnic particularism.[13]

Trilling's transcendent impulses were a pronounced version
of this tendency. Just as his radicalism was "rootless" and
faded quickly from his life, just as his Jewishness was for him
more an abstract signification than a burden or an honor, and
just as history was, for him, more lesson than experience, so
in general was the force of any sort of determinism diminished
as his career progressed.

Trilling's disengagement from the "particularism" and

"everydayness" of history issued also from another characteristic of American intellectual life as conditioned by the 1930's. Though that life had experienced political optimism followed by political disillusionment, it had also made an alliance of sorts with the literary modernism exemplified by such monumental (and unavoidable) figures as Proust, Eliot, Joyce, Kafka, and Mann. Thus it had been schooled in the ways that mundane happenstance could be rendered vulnerable, or even infinitely exploitable, by the manipulations of the pen. The literature of high modernism was, moreover, international, not provincial; its loyalties went only to where great talent and sensibility flourished; it saw every apparent "given," be it of belief or sympathy, loyalty or piety, as expendable. Modernism thus bore similarities to the destructiveness Marx and Engels had once claimed to be the particular property of Western bourgeois life. Modernism, like capitalism, had unleashed a fury in which everything stable was jeopardized: "All fixed, fast-frozen relationships with their train of vulnerable ideas and opinions are swept away, all new-formed ones become obsolete before they can ossify. All that is solid melts into air, all that is holy is profaned." *

For a while at least, some of the intellectuals of Trilling's generation believed that advanced political consciousness could happily be joined with this advanced literary or cultural consciousness. Both modernism and leftism, particularly anti-Stalinist leftism, were "radical"; both were on the frontiers of consciousness and energy. One repository of this confidence, the *Partisan Review*, emerging amid great editorial travail and controversy in 1937, was to represent the fusion of both advanced movements. For years, as *the* journal of Trilling's generation, it was able to keep that strange fusion alive. With the ministrations of editors like William Phillips and

---

*For a searching study of the relations of modernism to the Communist Manifesto and to communism in general, see Marshall Berman, "All That Is Solid Melts into Air: Marx, Modernism, and Modernization," *Dissent* (Winter 1978), pp. 54–73.

Philip Rahv, Trotsky could plausibly consort on the pages of the *Partisan Review* with, say, T. S. Eliot.

But Trilling knew that the union was contrived and fragile. Forced to choose between the elements comprising it, he preferred the modernism. In addition to its other glories, modernism let him see the world of politics as a lesser, mutable part of reality. Literary modernism seemed to be a magic wand itself: it could suddenly dismiss the world of day-to-day existence, find it drab, and say of its social conventions that they were only illusory. Trilling wanted always to be able, should the need arise, to associate himself with this advantage: to be at one with the ventilating power of a literary tradition holding itself superior to the material providing its "content." This does not mean that modernism could console him, or that he wrote to champion all its authors. Indeed, much modern literature distressed or dismayed him. But he turned to it as one would turn to an ally, for it signified removal. Just as Jewishness could not hold him, just as history and event could not hold him, so what one might call "pre-literary reality" could not hold him. Joyce's Dublin, he knew, was not *Ulysses*; Proust's Paris was not his art; Yeats had descended to "the foul rag-and-bone shop of the heart," but had not deposited his poetry there. What held ultimate power in Trilling's dialectical notion of the relationship between "reality" and "literary modernism" was the elevating force within the latter. It could embrace, subordinate, and go fairly far beyond everything it met.

But Trilling also knew that he was living in a time of political demands. Politics could be subordinated; it could not be dismissed. His responsibility as an intellectual was to provide a way to admit political reality into his thinking without conferring preeminence upon it. This is the gist of his celebrated comment in 1946 that we must "force into our definition of politics every human activity and every subtlety of every human activity. There are manifest dangers in doing this, but greater dangers in not doing it. Unless we insist that politics is imagination and mind, we will learn that imagination and mind are politics, and of a kind that we will not like."[14] The art consists of recognizing the full implications of politics while being always mindful of its secondary status. That art, one of intellectual diplomacy, is to be practiced while one's transcendence of historical detail and ethnic particularism is held firmly in mind. That these were, in part, self-imposed difficulties (Trilling *willed* his kind of transcendence) does not make them less complex. Reading Trilling, one is always aware of that complexity: he is of the American 1930's and of the generation of New York thinkers profoundly shaped by that decade's turmoil, yet he stands oddly aside from those times, and from his colleagues and their many intensities. His style—urbane and lambent, but never rapid, never aggressive —mirrors the oddness of his being engaged with the aggravations of modernity though never tormented by them. This gracious, full style is not that of someone victimized by modernism, but that of someone who acknowledges the full range of modernism's pressures while remaining conscious of the means to escape them. Trilling seems perpetually poised to depart, ready to leave behind or shed the constraints and filiations his kindred intellectuals saw as central.* Every reader of Trilling's essays knows how often he employed "we" as a pronoun to suggest a corporate intellectual involvement on his

*Alfred Kazin, in his memoir of Trilling in *New York Jew*, makes much of the difference between himself and Trilling as Jews: "For Trilling I would always be too Jewish, too full of my lower-class experience. He would always defend himself from the things he had left behind." Kazin enjoys his own phrase, saying elsewhere: "With his look of consciously occupying an important place, his already worn face of thought, his brilliant discriminations as we talked, [Trilling] quietly defended himself from the many things he had left behind." For Kazin, a vastly more sentimental and elegiac writer than Trilling, the older critic had "accommodated" himself to America. The son of an immigrant tailor, Trilling had "paid a price" for his culture; and that price seemed, to Kazin, much too high, for it was the very authenticity of his Jewishness. Kazin's speculations are no more than speculations, and his notion that the self "left behind" by Trilling was somehow more real and authentic than the one to be found in his writings seems to me idle and incorrect. There is no "better" Trilling than the one we have in his writings. See *New York Jew* (New York, 1978), pp. 46–47, 43, 192.

part; how many readers grasp the ambivalence with which he ultimately held this corporate identity? In contrast to those kindred intellectuals, to their affinity for the immediate struggle and the precise memory of the specific tension, Trilling turned always to the larger struggle and the larger tension. Thus he gave his mind over to the Self and to its dialectical drama amid Circumstance; he was attentive to history as an enactment of long-term implications, not short-term ones; he would rather have dwelled under the aspect of Western Civilization in its entirety than, say, in post-Depression times. He knew that in the long run we shall all be dead, and for that very reason pondered the ways the finality of death frames the moral questions of living. Here, and not here, engaged, but engaged in the most elaborately diffident of ways, Trilling is best read after conceding to him an expanded intellectual context. As a writer, he was not entirely of his time, or of his place.

3. The Fictions of a Self

THE PERSONAL SELF WAS TO BE, in its transformations and oppositions, an abiding concern for Trilling from the start of his writing career. That career began in 1925, when he was twenty years old, in the pages of *The Menorah Journal* (a publication, then ten years old, of the nonsectarian but broadly American Jewish Intercollegiate Menorah Association, whose managing editor from 1925 to 1932 was Elliot Cohen, later founder and editor of *Commentary* magazine).* For Trilling to have been found in the pages of *The Menorah Journal* was an early indication that his connection with the Jewish community in New York was to be sustained through its more secular, intellectual, and liberal spheres. His was not a Jewishness of the Yiddish language, or of Zionism, or of the flavor of Eastern Europe. Trilling in 1925, the year he graduated from Columbia College, wrote and had published in the *Journal* his first story, "Impediments."[1] Slight and now justly all-but-forgotten, it turns upon a central problem of modern identity that Dostoevsky (among others) had relentlessly examined, and that Saul Bellow was to make the subject of *The Victim* in 1947, and then to pursue in much of his later fiction. The

---

*In speaking at the funeral service for Cohen on May 31, 1959, Trilling called him "a man of genius" and "the *only* great teacher I have ever had." See "On the Death of a Friend," *Commentary*, 29, no. 2 (Feb. 1960), pp. 93–94. One part of that teaching genius was, for Trilling, "his sense of the subtle interrelations that exist between the seemingly disparate parts of a culture, and between the commonplaces of daily life and the most highly developed works of the human mind." Trilling's own career may be read as a pursuit of those interrelations. For background on the Intercollegiate Menorah Association and its magazine, see Alan M. Wald, "The Menorah Group Moves Left," *Jewish Social Studies*, XXXVIII, nos. 3–4 (Summer–Fall, 1976), pp. 289–320.

problem is that of the "double." The "double" is, in psychological terms, the unwanted or even intolerable part of the self
that is repressed but that nonetheless manages its own peculiar
assertions. In social terms, it is the negation of self that appears necessary if the individual is to take a place in the human community. In moral terms, the "double" represents
those longings of an illicit sort whose suppression can afford
one a sense of virtue. In any such fictional recreation as Trilling's, the self is made to meet its counterpart; the author is on
hand to establish the situation for the encounter or, as Trilling himself puts it in an epigraph by way of Shakespeare,
"Let me not to the marriage of true minds/Admit impediments. . . ."

In this early account, the writing self is made to acknowledge a certain Hettner: "I did not like the fellow, a scrubby
little Jew," for he might ". . . break down the convenient bar-
rier I was erecting against men who were too much of my own
race and against men who were not of my own race and hated
it. I feared he would attempt to win into the not-too-strong
tower that I had built myself. . . ." In this neat and small fictional formula, Hettner represents both the embarrassing Jew
within and the threatening anti-Semite without.* Both need
to be repelled: "I like people's outsides, not their insides, and
I was particularly reluctant to see this man's insides; they
would be, probably, too much like mine." The story is, after
these nervous and painful disclosures, not much more than

---

*In 1944, contributing to the *Contemporary Jewish Record* (the immediate
predecessor of *Commentary*), Trilling put forward with great frankness his
views on being Jewish and its value to him as a writer. Some of his remarks
have been quoted earlier. Here another is salient: "As the Jewish community
now exists, it can give no sustenance to the American artist or intellectual who
is born a Jew. And so far as I am aware, it has not done so in the past."
("Under Forty: A Symposium on American Literature and the Younger Generation of American Jews," *Contemporary Jewish Record*, VII, no. 1 [Feb.
1944], pp. 17, 15.) The attitude Trilling takes in this wartime Symposium is
that Jewishness either is negligible as a characteristic, or can evoke only "fear,
shame, attraction and repulsion." He thus feels as does the narrator in his
first story: Hettner is there, is all too present, and will not help and cannot
help.

formula. Self encounters self, and the meeting is rudely terminated with an insult from Hettner. The narrator, however,
feels victorious; his defenses have not been overrun. The double departs; the ritual has been methodically enacted and
carefully described.

It is a ritual, however, to which Trilling was to return in his
writing over the years. In his later fiction self is never far from
self, and the drama that makes up his fiction quite frequently
is that of an individual who achieves a partial kind of identity
at the cost of shouldering aside a kindred being. All of Trilling's carefully choreographed stories, and his one novel,
bring beings, or parts of beings, together. His energies are
thus spent largely in introductions and their consequences.
In 1929, he gave one explanation of why any Jewish writer
might find himself working in such a specialized manner. Reflecting on the various myths of the Jew that have been a
part of Western culture for centuries, Trilling said that the
Jewish writer "found the myths awaiting him. Sometimes he
fought them, sometimes he accepted them to his own advantage, often he went off and contemplated them in great confusion of mind. When he came to write of himself he was not
able to free himself of them. Some of them had become a
Doppelgänger of his, moving by the side of the real person we
suppose he must be."[2] That Doppelgänger moves ceaseless-
ly in and out of Trilling's fiction; we are never really to lose
sight of it. "Impediments" contains, moreover, a note sounded
many times again in that fiction, as well as in his criticism.
We see it first here, but it will become familiar as time goes
on: it is the idea that death presents itself to us as the best
reminder of life's genius, and as the most challenging adversary to life's transitoriness and mutability. Death has, for
Trilling, the grandeur of finality and the permanence that
only one other phenomenon—art—can match. In the 1925
story he writes: "Then, 'Death,' I said, 'is life's best pal and
severest critic. . . .' " Or, as he wrote in 1975, the year in which
he was to die:

All thought and art, all conceptual possession of the processes of life, even that form which we call love, has inherent in its celebration and sanctification of life some element of this negation of life. We seek to lay hold of the fluidity of time and to make perdurable the cherished moments of existence. . . . Art, even when it is at pains to create the appearance of intense and vigorous action, has the effect of transmuting that which is alive into that which has the movelessness and permanence of things past, assimilating it in some part to death.[3]

Death judges life, and does so with magisterial conclusiveness. Art also is magisterial and also concludes. Thus, in early fiction and late criticism, Trilling brings together, with remarkable diplomatic skill, forces otherwise to be thought at odds. Wholly to understand art is to appreciate how much it shares the stasis of death. Trilling's way of expressing this idea changes much from early writing to late—indeed, his style brings to itself over the years seriousness, then gravity, then solemnity, and even at last lugubriousness—but what does not change is the will on his part to reconcile aspects of selfhood. In this case the aspects to be reconciled are the mortal self that creates and the immortal self that can be located in art.

Trilling's early fiction follows him, or characters much like him, from New York to Wisconsin, where he taught for a year, then back to New York and Hunter College, where he taught in the evening session for two years before joining the faculty of Columbia University in 1932.* It is the fiction of a

*He was an instructor at Columbia from 1932 to 1939, assistant professor until 1945, associate professor from 1945 to 1948, and professor from 1948 on. From 1965 to 1970 he was the George Edward Woodberry Professor of Literature and Criticism; in 1970 he became a University Professor at Columbia, a position he resigned in 1974. He had, then, been involved with Columbia for more than fifty years, from his matriculation as an undergraduate in 1921 until his death. That Trilling's early career at Columbia was made difficult by anti-Semitic pressures within the institution is discussed by Sidney Hook ("Anti-Semitism in The Academy: Some Pages of the Past," *Midstream*, 25, no. 1 [Jan. 1979], pp. 49–54), and by Diana Trilling ("Lionel Trilling, A Jew at Columbia," *Commentary*, 67, no. 3 [Mar. 1979], pp. 40–46). They disagree about many details of the situation which at last, in 1939, brought Trilling an appointment as Assistant Professor of English, but they both say that the then President of Columbia, Nicholas Murray Butler, was instrumental in seeing to it that Trilling would be the first Jew so appointed.

young and anxiously introspective man. He writes, as do many young men, with an authority claimed but not completely earned. Some parts of self, of life, are not yet mastered. In one fragile story (the second he was to write), he describes a youthful Jew who embarrasses a sedate party by his manic desperations:

He began to feel not like a prophet come howling from the wilderness to warn a people defiling holiness, but like a satyr leaped into a respectable home . . . lustfully Hebraic, rowling gloriously, drunkenly, madly, in Jewishness, disgusting the inhabitants by the abandon and licentiousness of his Semitic existence. He smirked at himself: patriot by perversity.[4]

In yet another story, the outsider, an instructor at a midwestern university, studies with enormous attentiveness his own displacement. A Jew, "a stranger in a strange land," as Trilling puts it, he is required to offer formal acknowledgment of the fact that an older, gentile colleague has died. But to participate in such a ceremony is to remind himself of how much an "outsider" he himself is, and with what high and nervous regard for his own self he has taught himself to move among his colleagues:

. . . if he gives himself over to intercourse with mediocrity and out of politeness and diffidence says to mediocrity that it is nice, excellence will cease to know him.
    In fear, he had tried by simple means to effect an isolated integrity.
    . . . now had come to him this knowledge: that as a Jew, declared so, declared so to himself, he would be alone, apart, outside, free.

But such freedom carries with it the burden of inward suffering. So, declining at last to pay his respects, he detaches himself from his colleagues and, walking away, enters into his own bitterly familiar and unattractive consciousness:

The day had greyed to sternness; the wind that blew over the lake was silent and swift. The tiny sun was only a more luminous greyness, trivial. On such days one should set out on journeys, for then there is no brass band of brightness to make one forget whither one is going, nor for how long, nor the sort of company one can be to one's self.[5]

And a story of 1928, again placed in the midwest, and again turning with great care upon the decorous but febrile mind of a young instructor, treats with formulaic strictness its own stated subject. Once more, protagonist and Doppelgänger stand before us: "there were two aspects to Being a Jew: the Subjective and the Objective—What does it Mean to Be a Jew to Yourself and What does it Mean to Be a Jew to Others?"[6]

The Trilling of these stories writes with a "fastidiousness" and a "dignity," and even a "grace," that his former Columbia teacher Mark Van Doren noted.[7] He writes, however, with no particular power; his engagement with his self is unventilated and without perspective. Endowed with energy, but also constrained by authorial self-consciousness, these stories are now chiefly interesting by virtue of the fact that they announce concerns never to be laid aside by the more authoritative and capacious Trilling: the self, death, involvement with others and its costs, and the bitter pleasures of estrangement. Here the context is Jewish displacement; later the context will become general. Jewishness as a consideration will become blurred and the weight of its specificity will be lifted.

Two stories and a novel—"Of This Time, of That Place," "The Other Margaret," and *The Middle of the Journey*—come later and are clearly more substantial achievements.* They intensify Trilling's examination of the themes announced earlier, but do so with a force that commands the most serious consideration. Trilling will now take an aloof regard, and will not place himself under the direct scrutiny that had been the fate of narrators in the earlier fiction. Issues are now given motion by being made dialectical: characters take up positions and are arrayed against each other. The nar-

*A third story, "The Lesson and the Secret," published in *Harper's Bazaar* in March 1945, is negligible in comparison to "Of This Time, of That Place" and "The Other Margaret." Trilling apparently published no short fiction after 1945.

rator is detached and yet a participant; while the intense drama is played out on a small stage, he observes and suffers. While suffering, he learns. In these later fictions the engagements are more intense, the drama notably richer.

"Of This Time, of That Place," first published in *Partisan Review* in 1943,[8] is about the expense of spirit—more precisely the suffering—involved in teaching, in dealing with youthful promise. It is also about "madness." It examines a figure familiar to any of Trilling's readers: the protagonist who is unconfident but aspiring, conscience-ridden and grave. Given in this story the name "Joseph Howe," he is faced, as a college teacher, with two "mad" students: one is Ferdinand R. Tertan, who brings to him respect, a singular intelligence, and love; the other is Theodore Blackburn, who brings to him deception and callow ignorance. One sign of Howe's intelligence is that he recognizes the derangement of *both* students. Tertan is deeply troubled, "mad" in a clinical sense. As the story develops, he is sent to be examined by a physician and is to be sent away from the college at the end of the school term. He is brilliant, friendless, and disconsolately intellectual in ways that force from his company all his classmates. And he bears to his teacher a reverence so strong that Howe cannot fully absorb it. The sadness that pervades "Of This Time, of That Place" comes from Howe's gradual understanding of this inability on his part. Blackburn is "mad" in a wholly different, and wholly unclinical, sense. His is a madness approved by society; it will bring him success and acclaim. It is a madness derived from ambitiousness and a willingness to manipulate anyone standing in his path. Tertan's endearing genius comes from his total estrangement; Blackburn's offensiveness from his total involvement with society. The one represents the alienation, the other the socialization, of the human individual. The one "doubles" the other.

Thus far the story obeys a paradigm, one formally traced by Rousseau in his "First Discourse" and later studied by Freud: What does one give up on one's way to becoming a social being? What are the psychic costs of assimilation? What do we forfeit when we become "like the others"? Tertan's almost heroic stature in the story bespeaks the costs of not submitting to social demands, Blackburn's malevolent cheapness bespeaks the costs of total submission. This paradigm is central to Trilling's thought for the rest of his career. In Freud's *Civilization and Its Discontents*, treated in *Sincerity and Authenticity* (1972), the tragic circumstances not merely of solitary individuals but of entire societies involved in the process of submission and socialization are studied. In that later discussion, Trilling remarks upon the enormous tragedy of society itself. To be itself, and to maintain itself, society must offer sacrifices of great consequence out of its fund of primitive, singular, and brilliant integrity. For Freud, the fact of the matter is that it *must* do so; Trilling never disagrees with this conclusion, but adds to it, in all of his discussions, his own darkly tragic colorations.

Here the process is played out in a situation infinitesimal by comparison. We are given two college students, not society in a larger sense. The paradigm nonetheless has its force. Confronted with the socially assimilable, and the socially unassimilable, we are asked to calculate the expense of being each in turn. And we are asked to see that each, lying at one extreme of human behavior, demands to be treated with an understanding not free of pain. As Trilling later said, in thinking back to "Of This Time, of That Place," the story supports the notion that "there are kinds of insanity that society does not accept and kinds of insanity that society does accept."[9] Tertan is at the end institutionalized; Blackburn becomes the first in his class to find a most attractive job. The futures of both young men are thus decisively pre-established. Trilling, of course, wants his story to be considered as more than formula, and many years after its writing he argued convincingly that its power rests "in its ability to generate resistance to the certitude that Tertan is deranged."[10] But deranged he is; the certitude is a certitude. As readers we find the story compelling because in order to resist its paradigmatic truths we must feel that our (and Howe's) affection for Tertan is more important, and more valuable, than our rational understanding that he is, clinically speaking, ill. We want our affections, our own private emotional selves, to triumph over our rational and public selves. "The judgment of morality," as Trilling puts it, is in rivalry with the judgment "of science." [11] Thus, with the author's help, we may more fully appreciate the force of the last lines Tertan speaks in the story. As he looks at those whose peculiar and well-knit society he cannot join— the society of Howe, of Howe's dean, of Howe's landlady's daughter, and of the repellent Blackburn—he says, "instruments of precision." It is his cryptic, but absolutely unerring, way of judging those who will, collectively, judge him. They will, because they must, stand as a group to one side of Tertan, and with a scientifically valid "precision" they will cast him out. He, however, is superior to that precision and to the scene as a whole. And Howe, himself doubtful about precision, is left to ache with pity for Tertan's isolation. This immensely conservative ambivalence, on Howe's part, toward science, toward collective human judgment, toward the expensive process of human socialization, and toward rational and calculating modes of thought is characteristic of Trilling. He shares that ambivalence. It is what will grow to define him as a critic of literature and of society.

"The Other Margaret," published in *Partisan Review* in 1945,[12] takes as its theme the truth of a quotation from Hazlitt: "No young man believes he shall ever die." It is the story of a father who himself no longer feels young, who aspires to a real and unaffected wisdom, and who observes his young daughter falling victim to her own idealism. That idealism is expressed in social terms, in progressive or liberal thought. The daughter, Margaret, believes she comprehends the ills of the world and how they may be eased. People, she supposes, are victims of circumstances and are not responsible for their exploitation. The troublesome and petulant maid for the family, the "other" or "double" Margaret, is a case in point. She is to be explained and excused in light of the fact that " 'She has a handicap. Because she's colored. She has to struggle so hard—against prejudice. It's so *hard* for her.' " But Margaret's father believes none of this. His mind this day is on finalities, not on liberal notions. With Hazlitt in his head, he rises above questions of social melioration and sees all people as fated and yet responsible for those fates: "Exemption was not given by age or youth, or sex, or color, or condition of life." Talk about democracy and equality does not touch him at all, for he knows that death moves in ways vastly more "democratic" than any social forces his daughter might have in mind. He soberly reflects that in "the knowledge of death, all men were equal in their responsibility." Thus, when the "other" Margaret intentionally breaks a small and delicate object in sight of the idealistic Margaret, her father can offer her only small solace. His daughter weeps bitterly and uncontrollably. And she weeps, her father knows, not for the smashed object, but for her knowledge that the maid has indeed committed, purposefully, a malicious act. Her father also knows that "it was not the other Margaret but herself that his Margaret was grieving for, that in her foolish and passionate argument . . . she was defending herself from her own impending responsibility."

In this story, then, coming of age means, for Trilling's created characters and perhaps for himself, understanding what Hazlitt knew and what his exemplary young man did not. It means understanding that under the shadow of death, social melioration is no more than a fancy and personal responsibility is everything. *The Middle of the Journey* is to take up these concerns in their fullest amplitude. Both the story and the novel are to serve as fictional enactments of an abiding conviction on Trilling's part as he emerged from the late 1930's and the 1940's: that all political doctrines—but particularly liberalism in its heady notions of improvement, progressive change, and individual enhancement—are sus-

pect. Wisdom consists, as Margaret's father believes he discovers, in positioning oneself somewhere beyond the local and
the ephemeral. In fact, a familiarity with death, surely a great
leveler, is the one relationship that can assure a man a perspective from which he can judge well political vacuity. And
if these early writings are Trilling's fictional enactment of
such a belief, the essays he wrote in the 1940's and collected in
The Liberal Imagination are its explicit form.

4. The Middle of the Journey: Death and Politics

The Middle of the Journey has often been taken, for good reasons, as a "political" and a "liberal" novel. By this is commonly meant that we are to see in it, as Arthur Schlesinger, Jr., has said, "a searching and compassionate account of the liberal's dilemma of conscience in a world of absolutes." Daniel Patrick Moynihan, also much taken by the book, praised it as "a novel about the two great absolutist ideas of our time and the wan possibility of maintaining a distance from either."[1] Such understandings of the novel have their proper claims upon our attention, and few readers of *The Middle of the Journey*, written just after the Second World War and published in 1947, can free themselves of their memory of the book as a studiously crafted examination of the literary mind engaged in political complexities. That mind contrives its fictional realities as it holds in fixed positions some of the political possibilities of the day: communist, anticommunist, anti-anticommunist, liberal. Yet this understanding of Trilling's achievement can also temper one's admiration for it. Must the novel, one asks, be so claustrophobically paradigmatic? Must it, for all its elegance, be determined to air certain issues of the time in so deliberate and chaste a way? These misgivings are reinforced by some facts surrounding the composition of the novel. They support the reader's sense of *The Middle of the Journey* as an elaborate design that, in its fullness and delicacy, has a design upon him. In explaining the peculiarly important function that one character, Gifford

Maxim, came to have in the novel, Trilling wrote in 1975 that Maxim was perfectly appropriate to his "polemical" intention. That intention was one of ". . . bringing to light the clandestine negation of the political life which Stalinist Communism had fostered among the intellectuals of the West."[2] This was not to be the whole of the novel—indeed, it has, I believe, a more general and grave ambition, to which we will presently turn—but surely the function of Gifford Maxim in the book was to cast the deep political shade of anti-Stalinism into every corner of the action. Trilling had seen clearly how Stalinism had damaged American writing in the 1930's. "Proletarian literature" had been the result, and to its predictable rigidities he opposed his whole being as a writer. Political reality was hardly so certain as such a literature had assumed.

As Trilling explained in 1975, the figure of Maxim had been based directly on Whittaker Chambers. By 1947, several years before the extraordinary hearings and trials involving Chambers and Alger Hiss, Trilling had known Chambers for twenty-three years. They had been students together, though not friends, at Columbia College.* And from Trilling's account of the relationship, one that evoked equal parts of respect and repulsion in him, we may see just how important Chambers was. Calling him a "tragic comedian of radical politics," and seeing in him a mixture of the absurd, the portentous, and the formidable, Trilling did not in fact start the novel with him in mind. Rather, he entered the story, we are told, "unbidden"; and Trilling goes on to say, in a decorous Jamesian way, that ". . . he must have been responding to an invitation that I had unconsciously offered."[3]

---

*Nowhere in Trilling's stately lucubrations alluding to Chambers can one fix precisely upon anything that might pass for a specific element in their friendship. For a more pointed look at how that friendship was maintained, and how, for instance, it involved directly and concretely discussions of such matters as social-fascism, Hitler, communism, the Comintern, etc., see Sidney Hook's "The Strange Case of Whittaker Chambers," *Encounter*, XLVI, no. 1 (Jan. 1976), pp. 81–82.

Whatever the reasons for his entry into the book, and those reasons obviously involved grave personal issues for Trilling, Maxim's place in it now overpowers certain of its other major considerations. In short, Maxim—or Whittaker Chambers— makes *The Middle of the Journey* a political *roman à clef* for many readers. The controversies still surrounding Chambers and Hiss, and even the origins of Richard Nixon's rise to power, seep unstoppably into readings of the book, giving it a melodramatic coloration and a mysteriousness it might otherwise never have had. Yet to the degree that the "case" keeps interest in the novel alive, so also, I believe, does it obscure its meaning.

The novel turns, in its complexity, upon death. Death initiates, conditions, and gives character to all of its main events. The people in the novel approach death in many different ways, and in their encounters with it invite understanding of their selves. Death delineates and judges them. Thus it stands central to everything, subsuming politics as it subsumes all other phenomena, but doing so with suppleness and never with the morbidity one might imagine it possessing.

Trilling tells us that before Maxim came "unbidden" into the composition of the novel it was to have been a "*nouvelle*," the theme of which would be explicit. It was, he writes, ". . . about death—about what had happened to the way death is conceived by the enlightened consciousness of the modern age."[4] And he implies, as we have seen, that this original theme was supplanted by the theme abruptly announced with the appearance of Maxim. Thus the primacy of death is overcome by the primacy of politics; Stalinism seizes centrality. Or so, almost thirty years after the publication of the novel, Trilling would argue. I would submit, however, that no such displacement actually occurred. Trilling, it would seem, was as awestruck in 1975 as many of the novel's readers over the years by the connections to be made between his character Maxim and Whittaker Chambers and, more dramatically, by the way in which a reading of the novel could now stimulate interest in the train of events in which Chambers participated. As the novel has become political in the most explicit and direct of ways, and as it has fed speculation about the "true" character of Chambers and even of Hiss and his wife, so Trilling himself seems to have become less attentive to the theme that originally set the book in motion. The simple *literary* fact of the matter, however, is that Maxim's position in the novel, though arresting, does not eclipse that larger consideration—death—around which Maxim, like everyone else, anxiously moves.

The Middle of the Journey can, I concede, never be seen as a purely *literary* object. It is now attached to history, a glass through which we may darkly view American communism and anticommunism. But as such a glass it is remarkably unhelpful. One does not learn much about politics, about communism, or even about anticommunism. One does learn that political passions may issue from minds incapable of genuine reflectiveness, and that partisanship of any sort can be at times but sadly partial. One learns that most political people are dwarfed, in some important respect, by their beliefs. One learns that political life can be *extreme* life. As the novel closes, the poignantly apolitical but nominally "liberal" protagonist, John Laskell, is confronted by two of his closest friends, the one a passionate friend of communism (but not yet a communist), Nancy Croom, and the other the by-now profoudly anticommunist Maxim. They are both angry at him, and Laskell knows why: "It was the anger of the masked will at the appearance of an idea in modulation" (p. 302).*
He is modulation; they, in different ways, are not and are political. The modulated sensibility, attentive in every conceivable way to the variegated face of life, is, as any reader of Trilling knows, something of rare and admirable distinction. Sought by few and attained by fewer, it signifies true virtue.

*All page references to *The Middle of the Journey* are to the original edition (New York: The Viking Press, 1947).

Neither the Crooms nor Maxim can cherish that sensibility. John Laskell alone can. Maxim, however, recognizes it for what it is and chooses to repudiate it. The Crooms, particularly Nancy, simply will not open themselves to its attractions. They only dimly perceive it, and blindly thrust it away from themselves. Complementing each other to make up the world of politics as Laskell, and Trilling, were to see it in the 1940's, they represent the twin forces whose dominance in the world seemed prepared to crush the few Laskells remaining: "If Arthur Croom was the man of the near future, Gifford Maxim was the man of the far future, the bloody, moral, apocalyptic future that was sure to come . . . now it was possible to hold Gifford Maxim and Arthur Croom in his mind with no awareness of contradiction at all" (p. 55). They do not, in one important sense, stand in contradiction in Laskell's thinking because, since his recent illness, he has occupied a station strangely cut off from the turbulent flux of existence and its antagonisms. Never actually seeking it, he has been given a way to neutralize conflicting desires—be they political, social, or conventionally moral. This illness, through the proximity to death it brought about, has taught him something new about the world of human desire and human will: it can be transcended. The lesson comes as he contemplates a rose in the hospital. His meditations upon the rose are not unlike those of William Blake considering the useless perfections of a sunflower:

He could become lost in its perfection, watching the strange energy which the rose seemed to have, for it was not static in its beauty, it seemed to be always at work organizing its petals into their perfect relation with each other. Laskell, gazing at it, had known something like desire; but it was a strange desire which *wanted* nothing, which was its own satisfaction (p. 15).

Laskell reflects on the sweet oddness of the contentment he receives from so slight a thing, entering as he does so into a "kind of fullness of being, without any of the nagging interruptions of personality" (p. 15). Illness verging on death brings him, unbidden, clarity, order, and a world purified of human impediment. William James, in *Varieties of Religious Experience*, described this state as "the salvation through self-despair, the dying to be truly born, of Lutheran theology, the passage into nothing of which Jacob Behmen writes. To get to it, a critical point must usually be passed, a corner turned within one. Something must give way, a native hardness must break down and liquify."[5] Later, immediately before making love with the strangely still Emily Caldwell, and releasing himself into her "biological intelligence," Laskell reflects aloud upon his hospital days and comes to see precisely their attraction for him: "Yes, he insisted, he had been in love with death." Or, in the words of his perceptive nurse, Miss Paine, he had been luxuriating in an "affair" with death: "Quite a love affair with that flower, Paine had said. Quite a love affair with non-existence. That involvement with the rose, that desire that wanted nothing—what was it if it was not the image of death? Or, if not of death, then of not being born, which is but the gentler image of death. It was not quite extinction that he had taken such a fancy to, but it was something just short of extinction. It was the removal of all the adverse conditions of the self, the personality living in nothing but delight in itself" (pp. 25–26).

Later in his career Trilling was to dwell on these ontological conceptions, and, with phrases such as "sentiment of being" borrowed from Wordsworth, was to draw our attention to the nature and limits of pure self extracted from the merely circumstantial. In all such reflections he is never far from the recognition of simple mortality, and of the ways in which the meditative sensibility can move easily and swiftly from an enhanced sense of the plenitude and perfection of natural living things to an enhanced sense of the perfect absences alone offered by death. In this respect he is at one with Freud, who asked when we might "reform and give truth its due. Would it not be better to give death the place in actuality and in our thoughts which properly belongs to it, and to yield a little more prominence to that unconscious attitude towards death which we have hitherto so carefully suppressed?"[6]

On his recuperative visit to the Crooms, Laskell carries the knowledge of his meditative sensibility. It is exactly this knowledge he cannot communicate to them. Their youth is, in fact, defined by their willed ignorance of death. Nor can they discuss death as a subject; it is a fit topic neither when Laskell begins his visit at summer's start nor when he leaves them at its end: "They withdrew themselves in a polite, intelligent, concerted way whenever Laskell mentioned it. . . . They simply, in a sensible modern way, paid no attention at all" (p. 75). What they do instead, Laskell believes, is to make unfavorable comparisons between him, with his dark and threatening knowledge, and Duck Caldwell, who possesses the rude and vigorous manliness often attributed to the working class. One represents the disquieting fragility of mortal man, the other the plain and energetic hardihood upon which political struggles, it is often believed, are to be based. Thus, when Laskell is at last able to confront Nancy Croom and tell her that he has long wanted to speak about his illness and about the death of his former lover, he says: "you talk about morbidity and living in the past—as if you thought that death was politically reactionary" (p. 112).

And so it is for Nancy. Along with Margaret of "The Other Margaret," she shares the belief, rather anxiously defended, that there are certain worldly finalities upon which it is useless for the progressive mind to dwell. Since she believes that man is "dialectically" developing and that his potentialities are without limit, and since she also hopes that "eventually we will be able to change man's nature" (p. 108), it is more important to overwhelm the presence of death by energy than to recognize it with open passivity. Indeed, believing as Nancy believes is a process ultimately drawing more upon the powers of will than upon those of reflection. Hers is truly a made-up world, constructed equally of desire and forced ignorance. Thus, when Laskell comes at last to draw up conclusions

about his friends, he says of Nancy that she has "a passion of
the mind and will so pure that, as it swept through her, she
could not believe that anything that opposed it required consideration" (p. 233).

As much, then, as death informs this novel, will is present
to oppose death. In Trilling's sense of priorities in a complex
and mutable world, however, will is a lesser, yet more dangerous, force. It is what people have recourse to when they wish
to evade recognition of that end toward which we are all
traveling. All too unhappily human, it is a sign of desperation, a refusal to accept a certain elemental aspect of one's self.
It is the very opposite of "the desire that wanted nothing"
that had descended upon Laskell in the hospital and had
made him speculate on being, pure being, being without particular qualifications. The historian Philippe Ariès has spoken
of the ways in which the fervencies of the modern will have
sought, for ulterior social reasons, to suppress death. To be
engaged in society actively is to

> . . . avoid—no longer for the sake of the dying person, but for so-
> ciety's sake, for the sake of those close to the dying person—the
> disturbance and the overly strong and unbearable emotion caused
> by the ugliness of dying and by the very presence of death in the
> midst of a happy life, for it is henceforth given that life is always
> happy or should always seem to be so.[7]

Nancy Croom is, in this sense, preeminently a person with a
modern sensibility.

The sensibility of Gifford Maxim is anything but modern.
He is, as we have seen, "of the future," and his vision is violently apocalyptic, but he is also of the past in so far as the past
harbors notions, or involves forces, that it is the business of the
bright, progressive present to repel. The experience of the
past, in one of its simpler lessons, tells us that we must all die;
the present, though it grudges its assent to such a proposition,
encourages us to live otherwise. But Maxim, post- or premod-
ern, is described by Trilling as someone who "liked always to
have a reminder of death to make his work easier" (p. 303).

His experience as a communist revolutionary with "special" responsibilities has brought him sharply to the recognition that people do die, that at times they die violently That awareness of death amid apparent security is something his traumatic history, not his active will, keeps nourished in him. He is no longer a revolutionary, but he can keep faith with certain cruel lessons of his revolutionary past. Each of those lessons has to do with the sort of finalities against whose very formulation and establishment Nancy Croom, in order to exist, must oppose herself. In arguing, then, with Laskell and with the Crooms—and by extension with modern sensibility in its entirety—Maxim sees his step from revolutionism to devout Christian asceticism as most decisive, but hardly improbable: "It is not so very hard. I am practiced in believing doctrine that is full of mysteries. I have, you know, been dealing with free-will and predestination and foreknowledge, in original sin and redemption, all under different names and with a different outcome for a good many years now" (p. 291).

In that sense, then, death *is* politically "reactionary"—or so Trilling would lead us to believe in this book. To be a responsible person, one is obliged to entertain all of the sobering finalities represented by death. Once they are entertained (and Laskell believes that Maxim has at some time entertained the fullest presence of death by actually killing someone himself), the possibilities for optimism enshrined by liberalism pale and then disappear. As the shrewd Maxim sees it, the world is essentially constituted of two human forces: one he represents, and it is to be defined by the word "necessity"; the other is left to Nancy to represent, and "liberty" defines it. Maxim's force invokes the harshest versions of Christianity, and never-ending guilt is its regimen. Nancy's force flees from necessity into hope and solicitude for the masses, for whom there shall be much freedom and no guilt whatsoever. Together these two absolutely contradictory forces will shape the world, or so Maxim, talking to Nancy, can proclaim: " 'I'm sorry—but we must go hand in hand. Let it be our open secret. You will preach the law for the masses. I will preach the law for the leaders. For the masses, rights and the freedom from blame. For the leaders, duties and nothing but blame, from without and from within. We will hate each other and we will make the new world' " (p. 305).

On this note of heightened rhetoric the drama of the novel ends. There is no question in Maxim's mind that the sort of liberal *via media* for which John Laskell stands is to be excluded from the political apocalypse he envisions. Laskell simply does not count. "The humanistic critical intelligence," as Maxim calls it, is weightless, vaporous; hence we may now understand more clearly what liberals as eminent as Schlesinger and Moynihan had in mind when they spoke of the liberal dilemma "in a world of absolutes."

We may, however, see a bit further than they saw. We may note the ways in which the cards turn out to be formidably stacked against Laskell, and how, as the novel comes to its rather operatic and pathetic close, the liberalism he represents has been given little chance to breathe. Maxim, speaking brilliantly and dominating a conversation in which he grants no quarter, passes a kind of death sentence on Laskell:

"You stand there now, thinking that you know us all, and disapprove of us all, and yet do not hate or despise us. You are being proud of that flexibility of mind. But it won't last, John, it's diminishing now. . . . It is the last time that you will see it. . . . The supreme act of the humanistic critical intelligence—it perceives the cogency of the argument and acquiesces in the fact of its own extinction." (Pp. 304–5.)

Against such force, such invective and prophecy, Laskell can offer little. He proposes to offer opposition, but finds he cannot. He mentions, cryptically, "ferocity," but Maxim is there to remind him that ferocity is unbecoming to the liberal sensibility. Indeed, to be ferocious in any way is to avail oneself of the passions on which Maxim and Nancy depend, each in different ways, and which it is the duty of transcendent liberals like Laskell to abjure. He also proposes his own "idea in modulation," his own free intelligence, as a counter to both Nancy and Maxim. This too lacks weight. As Robert Warshow pointed out in an early and brilliant review of the novel, Trilling (and Laskell) cannot win the day merely by opposing doctrine with doctrine: "the novelist's function is not to argue with his characters—or at least not to try too hard to win the argument."[8] That, we remember, is how the "proletarian writers" managed things. Maxim, bitterly shrewd and aware of Laskell's immobility, says to him: "Better wait for the resurrection, John" (p. 305).

There is much that Trilling and his creation Laskell share, but we would misread *The Middle of the Journey* if we saw Trilling really offering much more sympathy to Laskell than that offered to him, tepidly, by Maxim. Of character, Laskell has much that is fine; but it is not enough. Of doctrine, he is in dignified possession of an insufficiency. He therefore can score no victory as the novel closes; rather, he only discovers an exit through which, at summer's end, he may depart from the Crooms, and Maxim, and the disconsolate Caldwells, and the discussions on which he has left so many marks but in which his force has been so vulnerable. It has not, in fact, been his summer; it has been Maxim's. Driven, peculiar, impossible, and ravaged, Maxim maintains a bearing second to no one in the book. Laskell we might sympathize with, but it is Maxim who imposes himself on us. Even Laskell accedes to his presence, granting it a dignity: "And I want to tell you— maybe I should have mentioned it before—that I was struck by a kind of honorableness he still had, even though he did desert the Party" (p. 182). As Irving Howe had seen, "Whenever Maxim speaks, the book is brilliantly alive." Laskell is, by contrast, just "a stick."[9]

Maxim's position seems comparable to that possessed by the actual figure on which Maxim was, in complicated ways, based. Whittaker Chambers seems to have had for Trilling some of the same imposing and uniquely honorable aspects of personality Maxim possessed. It was not Laskell, as we have seen, who rose so dramatically in Trilling's recollections of the novel in 1975. Nor did the Crooms then receive much mention; doctrinaire liberals of their sort had become no more than a benign category. It is Maxim/Chambers who returns with pressure and significance. Unbidden in the writing, and, almost thirty years later, forcing himself into memory, Chambers stood for Trilling as "a man of honor" (p. 19) whose "magnanimous intention" (p. 24) cannot be doubted. The "liberalism" of this novel, then, is at best a piety. Precariously maintained, and made uneasy in the presence of another force that mixes intelligence, aggressiveness, and a strange honor in shrewd proportions, it exists only to be threatened. It finds its solace in reflections upon death, and with death in mind it judges the effusions of political passion stridently surrounding it. Trilling's loyalty to such liberalism is odd and diffident. Perhaps the nature of that loyalty is one sign of the malaise and discomforts of political engagement in the 1940's in the United States. That so important a university intellectual in that "haunted" postwar time could put forward as a protagonist such a figure as John Laskell, and yet offer him such frail support in his contests of mind and will, reveals that even the more skeptical forms of liberalism had been placed under great stress. Liberalism in that time was provisional and wary. After the war, and after the bitter ashes of leftist engagement with the Soviet Union had been tasted, the open innocence of liberalism had gone. In sympathetic response to the new fate of liberalism, Trilling was bringing to a dark time his own dark reservations about politics. Conditioned by the enormous crudities of Stalinism to be both philosophically and emotionally wary in the face of possible political involvements, Trilling had well prepared the face that was to meet other faces in a cautious decade. He was, elaborately, ready for the 1950's.

5. The Lesson of Matthew Arnold and the Lessons of Mass Culture

LET US RECONSIDER the terms employed by Robert Warshow in his criticism of *The Middle of the Journey*. Warshow quite rightly saw that Trilling's identification with Laskell in that novel is unmistakable. He saw also that Laskell is called upon by Trilling to reject the ideas about life and politics represented on the one hand by Maxim and on the other by Nancy Croom. Trilling has Laskell say that "an absolute freedom from responsibility—that much of a child none of us can be. An absolute responsibility—that much of a divine or metaphysical essence none of us is" (p. 301). Laskell turns from both extremes and is, himself, "an idea in modulation," the very thing they cannot tolerate. Although Warshow is sympathetic to Trilling (and is later to gain Trilling's admiration),* he is determined to show that Trilling's diffident responses to the era's political demands represent a weakness. He says that Trilling has been "finally reduced to the level of his subject; like the Stalinists themselves, he can respond to the complexity of experience only with a revision of doctrine."[1] He goes on to say, as I remarked in the preceding chapter, that a novelist cannot hope to triumph if he puts himself into the position of arguing with his characters and, at least on the page, appearing to win over them. Something else is needed.

*See Trilling's "Introduction" to the collection of Warshow's essays and reviews, *The Immediate Experience: Movies, Comics, Theatre, and Other Aspects of Popular Culture* (Garden City, N.Y., 1962), pp. 11–22. He there says: "His work seen whole and in retrospect has a fineness of temper and tone and a degree of actuality which make it unique in its time" (p. 19).

Warshow delivered his criticism with precisely this contention in mind: something else was needed after Stalinism, or in the face of continuing Stalinism, in the 1940's and 1950's. Lionel Trilling, he thought, could be considered one of those intellectuals most fully alive to the complexities, the bitter ironies, and the nasty confusions of a political age bent severely by leftist totalitarianism. Trilling should have known, as "proletarian" writers, zealous American Communists, and some fellow travelers would not have known, what it meant to maintain an independent life of the mind amid such disorienting pressures. And yet Trilling's novel seemed inadequate to the challenge. It possessed a tendentiousness of its own, and it seemed, where it was not tendentious, dismayingly mild.

Warshow's criticism seems to me just. It also seems another of the countless legacies of Stalinism.* Warshow wanted something of *The Middle of the Journey* that, fine and poignant literary creation though it be, it could not give him. But could any novel? So great had the force of Stalinism been in the 1930's and 1940's—with its "fronts," edicts, positions adopted only to be revised, vast hopes carried and disappointed: with its way of inviting enormous loyalty and then of torturing loyalty beyond recognition by challenge mounted upon impossible challenge: with its virtues somehow superior to honesty and integrity, its fraudulent trials, and its murders—that intellectuals like Warshow felt the need for a countervailing force as distinct and powerful as the one they reviled. Merely to *think* Stalinism wrong was a feeble exercise.

The problem is nothing so simple as Stalinism; as I said before, that issue is settled: Stalinism today is not a point of view but a psychological and sociological phenomenon.

---

*Perhaps the single best study of the effects of Leninism and Stalinism on the intellectual community of the West is David Caute's *The Fellow Travellers: A Postscript to the Enlightenment* (London, 1973). Caute's extensive survey covers European, English, and some American writers and thinkers. His own viewpoint, however, is difficult to grasp: he is censorious toward both left and right, and seems unexcited about moderation.

. . . The intellectual's problem is to define his own position in the whole world of culture that came into being in the 30's—a world in which he must live and of which he is a full partaker. And the question to be asked is not: What is my opinion of all this? That question is easily answered, but those who ask only that have fallen into the trap, for it is precisely the greatest error of our intellectual life to assume that the most effective way of dealing with any phenomenon is to have an opinion about it. The real question is: What is my relation to all this?[2]

"What is my relation to all this?" The proper response, then, was not simply to establish an opinion, nor to work up an attitude, but to come to an understanding of one's experience, to assemble a vocabulary proper to that experience, and to set forth a fusion of experience and language such that the lethal force of Stalinism could, with strength, be repelled. This was what Warshow was after when he asked: "How shall we regain the use of our experience . . . ?" It was what he wanted when he said that the modern intellectual "faces the necessity of describing and clarifying an experience which has itself deprived him of the vocabulary he requires to deal with it."[3]

To describe the task in as candid a fashion as Warshow does is, however, to reveal its difficulty. Such an enormous struggle is ultimately a quixotic one. The irreducible fact of the matter is that even for intellectuals, Stalinism in the American 1930's was not just an intellectual force. It had currency in the American mind because it had real existence—economic, military, diplomatic, and political—in a foreign country of great potential power. Hence, for an American intellectual like Warshow to have wished to oppose Stalinism, the socialism of one vast nation, or to move beyond it, by mind alone, was to have been mistaken about its material existence. For some Americans in these troubled decades, its force might have seemed wholly "psychological and sociological." But its historical identity did not then reside within such confines, and truly to have stepped beyond those confines would have required something other than a redefinition, however profound, of one's relation to them. Rethinking was not enough. Stalin, and Russia, existed; they were not just products of thought.

But Warshow's efforts to disentangle himself from Stalinist history and its aftermath were nonetheless laudable. To understand that he had been given *his* history, and no other; to understand that the very terms current in the day were suspect because of their historical connections; to understand that one must recover a language and a sensibility proper to the real situation of the time—these were Warshow's working assumptions. They were also Trilling's. Beginning with his lengthy study of Matthew Arnold in 1939, Trilling's writing was a creative effort to know his present circumstances and to judge their defects, to know both current inadequacies and past achievements. His literary and cultural criticism is a reflection of how strongly he felt about both.

Let us examine, then, Trilling's most important work of the 1930's, the study of Matthew Arnold. To do so is not a particularly easy task, and the problem begins with Arnold himself. Certain attitudes and phrases, well known to all readers of Arnold, and greatly valued by Trilling, are not likely to possess much gravity or appeal to readers now. They seem gray and worn. To say that literature is "a criticism of life," or that one has an obligation "to see the thing as in itself it really is"; to maintain that a thinking person must acquaint himself with "the best that has been known and said in the world, and thus with the history of the human spirit," and that he must, following Montaigne, be *"ondoyant et divers"* in his pursuit of "sweetness and light"; to declare that "one gains nothing on the darkness by being . . . as incoherent as the darkness itself," and that "civilisation is the humanisation of man in society"; to believe that life must be affirmative, interesting, complete, and human, and that though order and liberty are both good, the one cannot provide the other—all of this is central to Arnold, and yet is unseductive. It is also central to Trilling. And it has made Trilling appear in some

quarters, both in the late 1930's and thereafter, an unseductive, old-fashioned man of letters.

That Trilling came to Arnold in the mid-1930's and found
him a source of great power and solace might now appear unlikely. To Trilling himself it once seemed so. But in writing
about Edmund Wilson, he recounts how important the engagement with Arnold proved to be. He also recounts how
Wilson encouraged that engagement:

At that time "everybody" was involved in radical politics in one
degree or another, and Wilson himself was a controversial figure
because of his famous statement, made in an essay of 1932, "A
Plea to Progressives," that we—that is, the progressives or liberals
—should take Communism away from the Communists. I was
trying to write a book about Matthew Arnold and having a bitter
time of it because it seemed to me that I was working in a lost
world, that nobody wanted, or could possibly want, a book about
Matthew Arnold. . . . I was much ashamed of what I had undertaken. But Wilson asked me how my book was getting on, and
not merely out of politeness but, as was clear, because he actually
thought that a book on Matthew Arnold might be interesting
and useful.[4]

The incident tells us something about Wilson's wide diversity of interests, and perhaps something about the character of
his detachment from radical politics.* Wilson could be both
of and not of those politics; he could write the nonpolitical
Axel's Castle in 1931 and then, in 1940, the political *To the
Finland Station*. He could, in other words, encourage the
younger Trilling to write of "a lost world" just when he was
most involved in the here and now. More to our purposes, it
tells us something about the ways in which, over the years,
Trilling patiently developed a mind that could oppose the
Stalinist mind. He knew that "everybody" at that time (and
in those small, fierce circles) was involved in radical politics;
the official left, monitored or controlled by the Soviet Union,

*For Wilson's laudatory review of the Arnold book, see "Uncle Matthew,"
New Republic, 98 (Mar. 22, 1939), pp. 199–200.

held sway; "fellow-traveling" was a serious and fashionable business. Yet Trilling reached out, not to the writing of a "proletarian" novel put together in the crude and formulaic way of an Albert Maltz or a Clara Weatherwax, nor to southern sharecroppers or the organizers of a textile strike, but to the lost world of Arnold. In concluding the distinguished book that resulted, he wrote: "Arnold's whole career had been spent in evaluating the French Revolution and if this seems small distinction in a century whose whole effort was to accommodate itself to that event, it is nevertheless true that Arnold worried the problem more constantly and explicitly than his contemporaries and was less satisfied with the simple answers."[5]

By transposition, we may say that Trilling's whole career as a critic was spent in evaluating Stalinism and its odd, but strong, vestigal remains, and that he "worried" the problem more constantly and explicitly than most of his contemporaries, being far less satisfied than any of them with the simple answers. One "answer" that apparently never satisfied him, but for some time satisfied others, was a political one: Trotskyism. This was the tendency of Marxism to which many American intellectuals, among them disaffected communists, permanent renegades, and other leftist pilgrims, were to adhere in the late 1930's and in the 1940's. Compared with Stalinism, and in light of conditions in the Soviet Union, it seemed to them more sophisticated, less coercive, more intellectual, more sympathetic to the arts. It became for them the brave dissident tradition of the left. Trilling's sympathies, though not his active energies, were with this tradition. He could go but halfway to Trotskyism because his mind was always to be riveted on the problems that grow out of a *literary* concern with social ills. His political place, blurred though it may have been in those times, was nevertheless with those who had broken with Soviet Communism in 1936–37 and considered themselves Trotskyists. Unlike some of them, he had never been a follower of the Communist Party in this country and he consequently never had suffered the trauma of "breaking." But his sympathies were inclined toward individuals some of whom had broken the connection. They included the editors, Philip Rahv and William Phillips, of the reformulated *Partisan Review*, and, among others, Sidney Hook, James Burnham, Lionel Abel, Louise Hacker, Dwight Macdonald, James T. Farrell, John Chamberlain, and Max Eastman. Sympathetic though he was with the thinking of such people, it was a sympathy extended from afar.* Trilling's political loyalties were born not out of engagement, but out of remote mediations. For these reasons, he was never really a "radical."

His more abiding concern, like Arnold's in England, was with the phenomenon of the middle class that surrounded him, in New York and elsewhere in the country. In his essay "Irish Catholicism and British Liberalism," Arnold had brought to succinctness one of his primary beliefs: ". . . the great work to be done in this country, and at this hour, is not with the lower class, but with the middle. . . ."[6] Every reader of Arnold is familiar with this sentiment.† It is, of course, at the heart of *Culture and Anarchy*. Arnold pursued it his whole life. In 1939, it was Trilling's turn to say the same thing:

My own literary interest . . . is in the tradition of humanistic thought and in the intellectual middle class which believes that it continues this tradition. Nowadays this is perhaps not properly pious; but however much I may acknowledge the historic role of the working class and the validity of Marxism, it would be *only*

*One of his few direct political involvements of the time was signing an open letter denouncing American members of the Communist Party for breaking up a Madison Square rally in 1934 honoring Austrian Social Democrats defeated by the regime of Chancellor Dollfuss (see Walter Goodman, *The Committee: The Extraordinary Career of the House Committee on Un-American Activities* [New York, 1968], p. 38n.).

†In 1879 he had said much the same thing: ". . . in the rule of this immense class, this class with so many correspondences, communications, and openings into the lower class, lies our future." See "Ecce, Convertimur ad Gentes," in Arnold, *English Literature and Irish Politics*, ed. R. H. Super (Ann Arbor, Mich., 1973), p. 9. This example is but one of many.

piety for me to say that my chief literary interest lay in this class and this tradition. What for me is so interesting in the intellectual middle class is the dramatic contradiction of its living with the greatest possibility (call it illusion) of conscious choice, its believing itself the inheritor of the great humanist and rationalist tradition, and the badness and stupidity of its action.

. . . it is for this intellectual class that I suppose I write.[7]

For a critic to align himself in the middle and late 1930's not with the working class then thought by many intellectuals to be richly endowed with bright future prospects, but with the middle class that was in every way boring and suspect, typifies Trilling's odd bravery. In some quarters, it made of him an embarrassing figure. Trilling himself, however, was not embarrassed. After all, Arnold had enjoyed the same fate in times not completely different. The attractions of revolution were felt to be pulsing as both men wrote. And both were forced to learn that there are few tasks less attractive than to see the middle class, from which they and their colleagues and friends come, as it is, and not as it imagines itself to be. The difficulty resides, Arnold and Trilling understood, as much in how to praise the real virtues of that class as in how to censure its obtuseness. In the United States before the Second World War, that class was uneasy about its strengths; and it allowed itself to be denigrated too easily for its weaknesses. It was shy and compliant. For all of that, however, it was a massive force. In nineteenth-century England, the strength was present, but not the compliance. The English blindness of the time consisted of its inflated sense of itself. Arnold's career was spent in criticizing that inflation. Of the size, the weight, and the consequent influence everywhere to be felt of their respective middle classes, then, Trilling and Arnold never lost sight.

In the years immediately following the heavy waves of oppression in the Soviet Union characterized by the "Moscow Trials," and in the period immediately during and after the Civil War in Spain, Trilling recognized that though the political writing on the wall was clear, and though many American fellow-travelers, having read it, were moving away from their devotion to official Soviet Communism, the news elsewhere was discouraging. Middle-class intellectuals might recognize stark political reality: about cultural reality even some of the more acute, even some of the Trotskyists, were likely to be confused. The cultural effects of a political passion were, Trilling sensed, to be felt long after the passion itself had cooled. Thus, though "Proletarian Literature" as a movement had largely spent its force, and though its death certificate had been issued by Philip Rahv in 1939 (he saw it, rightly, as the "literature of a party disguised as the literature of a class"),[8] the notion of a sacred power residing within the sensibility and will of the proletariat had not died away. It still conditioned the anxious beliefs of middle-class intellectuals; it still permitted them to misjudge, wildly, aesthetic quality; it still encouraged their covert anti-intellectualism; and it still supported their willed disfranchisement from the class to which they happened to belong. Some of these intellectuals still yearned to throw in their lot with those they saw as the truly dispossessed. The whole business of proletarian involvement was, to Trilling, an excellent contemporary example of what Arnold had years before called "philistinism." Writing in 1939, therefore, about the ways in which the literature of the 1930's was still in the ascendancy for that middle class, Trilling said that it has ". . . provided what is nothing less than a culture and an ethics . . . a code of excited humanitarianism . . . a subtle flattery by which the progressive middle-class reader is cockered up with a sense of his own virtue and made to feel that he lives in a world of perfect certainties in which critical thought or self-critical feeling are the only dangers."[9]

Trilling thus recognized one of the major social and cultural dramas of his time. He saw how a class might wish to will itself out of existence. He saw how it might, impelled by guilt, repudiate its own traditions. In part, of course, this drama was the result of a moral fashion and was thus, as Trilling was later to say, just a "moral anomaly."[10] But the fashion and the anomaly were to characterize American intellectual life in those years. The disequilibrium caused in the minds of those who, moved by guilt, sought to fashion a firm aesthetics and a firm politics out of a connection with the proletariat had not proven particularly helpful in either art or politics. The actual result, as Trilling saw, was intellectual pain and confusion. Such pain and confusion might prove interesting to some detached observer at some later time, but for those currently weighed down by them, they were severely damaging. For an intellectual to risk the emotional and intellectual securities of his own class position by opposing the prejudices of that class was a recurring phenomenon in the 1930's. Its force had hardly been spent by the end of the decade.

The attempt to evacuate a whole social class had, of course, classic leftist motivations. "The Manifesto of the Communist Party" states:

In times when the class struggle nears the decisive hour, the process of dissolution going on within the ruling class, in fact within the whole range of old society, assumes such a violent, glaring character, that a small section of the ruling class cuts itself adrift, and joins the revolutionary class, the class that holds the future in its hands. Just as, therefore, at an earlier period, a section of the nobility went over to the bourgeoisie, so now a portion of the bourgeoisie goes over to the proletariat, and in particular, a portion of the bourgeois ideologists, who have raised themselves to the level of comprehending theoretically the historical movement as a whole.[11]

This prophecy, or injunction, inspired (and deluded) thousands in the United States during the 1930's. Not the least of Trilling's achievements, effected with proper Arnoldian modesty, was to remind the intellectuals of the middle class that their class could not be evacuated, and that their individual departures from it were likely to partake not of Marxist glory, but only of grotesqueness. Trilling believed strongly that any such pilgrimages would yield nothing. In his own accounting of contemporary literary history, he had difficulty, in fact, in granting any substance at all to the much-vaunted "literature of the thirties." In 1946, for instance, he provided a historical account of recent American literature that simply left out what in the minds of so many other people had been a period of rich productivity: "It is now more than twenty years since a literary movement in this country has had what I have called power. The literary movement of social criticism of the 1920's is not finally satisfying, but it had more energy to advance our civilization than anything we can now see, and its effects were large and good. No tendency since has had an equal strength."[12]

Along with Arnold, then, Trilling believed that the true life of the mind could be maintained only by those who rooted themselves in the cultural origins they inwardly knew they could not deny. Knowing oneself meant, for Arnold and Trilling, obeying injunctions that involved the social as well as the purely ideological. It meant that one recognized, however deflating the recognition might be, the "conditioned," the unavoidable, the circumstantial. All of this was the more extraordinary in Trilling's situation because of the way he had, much earlier in his career, intricately negotiated a passage away from the "circumstantial" fact of his birth as a Jew. We have learned already how he would not be wholly of his time or of his place. Now we may see how, being made of contraries, he would devote himself to givens and to circumstances. For Arnold, and for Trilling at this stage, a careful and precise recognition of exactly what the "conditioned" might be in any cultural situation was an achievement of the highest order. To study the "conditioned" as literature records it and reproduces it was, in fact, one of Trilling's characteristic methods as a literary critic. Another, just as evident, was to detach himself from "conditions."

Here he recognizes them, but to recognize givens is not simply to praise what one is. One's class is not one's virtue; it is simply, indelibly, a central aspect of one's identity. Arnold did not celebrate the middle class; he accepted it for what it was and then went about scrutinizing it. He never believed he could will it out of existence. Trilling's procedure was the same. Writing of Arnold, Trilling called him a "culture hero." He thought of him as "a man who gives himself in full submission and sacrifice to his historical moment in order to comprehend and control the elements which that moment brings."[13] Disliking much of what the middle class was, Arnold nevertheless thought that it would "take the leadership in the next great events of culture and politics." And Trilling knew that Arnold had "wished to reform and enlighten it for the right performance of its historic role."[14] From the essays collected in *The Liberal Imagination* (1950) on to *Mind in the Modern World* (1973), Trilling's ministrations are carried on with the same assumption. Arnoldian lessons were never to be more respectfully assimilated.

The one teacher, however, is not the other. There is a note struck by Arnold, particularly in the middle of his life, that finds no correspondence in the work of Trilling. In reflecting upon it, Trilling calls it "banter"—but he could not have been too happy with it. It comes in 1864, in Arnold's *French Eton; or, Middle Class Education and the State*, where he envisages a perfect State, standing above all classes and resolving all contradictions. It will be no less than the middle class perfectly transformed into its best self: "raised to a higher and more genial culture," made "strong by its numbers, its energy, its industry, strong by its freedom from frivolity," and liberalized "by an ampler culture, admitted to a wider sphere of thought, living by larger ideas, with its provincialism dissipated, its intolerance cured, its pettiness purged away." Seeing all this in his mind's eye, Arnold concludes with an effusion: "Then let the middle class rule, then let it affirm its own spirit, when it has thus perfected itself."[15]

This kind of utterance is wholly foreign to Trilling. From the very beginning of his career, he has the most serious mis-

givings about the culture and the class to which he directs his
meditations. The reality of that class and culture is large and
unavoidable; its significance is awesome; its potential is massive. It must be recognized and accommodated to one's thinking. But such a class and such a culture reveal to Trilling no
signs within them of a higher synthesis yet to come. If there
is a higher self to which, in affirmation and perfection, they
may move, they have given no hint of it. In fact, a contrary
process is, to Trilling, all too evident:

For some decades now, that part of the middle class which
protests has been losing its love of society, which, as it feels, has
betrayed it. We have all in some degree become anarchistic.
Sometimes the anarchism takes the form of admiration of or
acquiescence in extreme forms of authoritarianism; a large part
of the intellectual, liberal bourgeoisie no longer dislikes authoritarianism if only it is not called by its right name. More often
our anarchism takes the more diffused form of disgust with the
very idea of society. On the upper levels of our taste this disgust
is expressed for us by Baudelaire, Rimbaud, Céline, and Kafka;
on a lower level of taste by the details of our middle-grade fiction; and we can of course see the continuation of this taste for
disgust in the popular and commercial art of our time.[16]

Thus Trilling in 1949. Arnold's optimism is never his.
With characteristic chronological vagueness ("for some decades now") Trilling sketches the outlines of something he
was beginning to see as a modern contagion. Middle-class culture is not bringing itself together. Without coherence, it
moves by extremes toward both absolutism and revulsion.
Threatening always to break down, it projects for itself no
higher self, no antithetical being out of which a reformed
order and higher balance may arise. It simply wars, unpro-
ductively, with itself.

These anxieties on Trilling's part are never to leave him.*

*An early sign of Trilling's awareness that the life of the mind was to be
spent in constant ambivalence amid the world's values is given in comments
on Ernest Hemingway: " . . . the artist must accept his culture and be accepted by it, but also—so it seems—he must be its critic, correcting and even
rejecting it according to his personal insight. . . . " See "Hemingway and His

Later he is to focus more intensely on the ways in which disgust is expressed by the "upper levels" of taste as they traffic with Céline, Kafka, and Baudelaire. He is to think of this traffic as an "adversary culture" operating within the very cells and tissues of the larger culture, and he is to become gloomily irritated at the prospects of the deterioration caused by it. He is also to remark, in passing, on the unresponsiveness and the flatness of much modern "middle-brow" fiction (see, for instance. "The Novel Alive or Dead," 1955),[17] and is to have only mild hopes that the novel, so substantially a product and part of middle-class aspirations, can give to that class any structure or coherence. The example of John Steinbeck's popularity serves him, again and again, as a forceful reminder of how dreary the present situation had become. About the popular and commercial art surrounding him he was to echo the very sentiments, most of them bitter, that almost every critic of mass culture was then busily expressing. Mass culture was no culture at all, but a substitute for culture. More precisely, it was a cancer taking up residence within genuine culture. Dwight Macdonald was to make part of a career out of his exacting study of such a phenomenon (see his *Against the American Grain, Discriminations,* and many of his movie reviews), but it was Clement Greenberg who, early on, gave a famous description of the process. That process was to intrigue, even to mesmerize, many other contemporary intellectuals, Trilling among them. Greenberg had said: "The new urban masses set up a pressure on society to provide them with a kind of culture fit for their own consumption. To fill the demand of the new market, a new commodity was devised: ersatz culture, kitsch, destined for those who, insensible to the values of genuine culture, are hungry nevertheless for the diversion that only culture of some sort can provide."[18]

Critics," *Partisan Review,* VI, no. 2 (Winter 1939), p. 60. The maintenance of contradiction is indeed to become, for Trilling, the life of the mind.

The rise of kitsch was appalling; but, like other diseases, it had a power to fascinate. Much of the fascination on the part of Greenberg, Macdonald, and Trilling issued from their anxiety that "high" culture was simply to be eclipsed by the power of the new mutant form. "High" culture might itself become mutant. It would be forced, in order to exist, to become more exotic, more rarefied in its concerns, more marginal to the general interest. Such culture had, of course, never been "popular," but it had always found ways to thrive, through one or another form of patronage, within the "massness" of culture. But now patronage itself seemed somehow diminished, and hence the avant-garde's power to lead, to direct, to stimulate, seemed diminished. The connections and the subtle equilibriums necessary for middle-class culture, in both its higher refinements and its lower satisfactions, were endangered. As Greenberg put it:

No culture can develop without a social basis, without a source of stable income. And in the case of the avant-garde, this was provided by an elite among the ruling class of that society from which it assumed itself to be cut off, but to which it has always remained attached by an umbilical cord of gold. The paradox is real. And now this elite is rapidly shrinking. Since the avant-garde forms the only living culture we now have, the survival in the near future of culture in general is thus threatened.[19]

Trilling found these dark predictions very persuasive. He was inclined, moreover, to think that most of the disagreeable end products of ersatz mass culture would have their way. "High" culture, the avant-garde, would be eclipsed, the lower forms would take over, and mind itself would be threatened. At the same time, the avant-garde, for as long as it would be able to maintain a hold on existence, would become a more and more extreme, and more violently proposed, version of itself. In its own death throes, it would, in its disfigurations, turn to attack the culture and the audience remaining responsive to it.

These somber reflections, cast again and again during Trilling's career, indicate how, as a follower of Arnold, he was nevertheless obliged to pursue a course of thought ultimately dissimilar to Arnold's. Paraphrasing closely Arnold's 1879 lecture and essay "Ecce, Convertimur ad Gentes," Trilling says that Arnold puts forward the notion that the hopes of the proletarian class ". . . are in every way justified but can be gained only by the middle class developing a civilization into which the workers can 'grow.' "[20] Both the proletarian hopes and the prospects for middle-class civilization are thus seen, by Arnold, as reasonable, and the relationship between the two groups is assumed to be compatible. Arnold knew that the British middle class of the nineteenth century was indeed "drugged with business,"[21] that "Economic Man" threatened to be a disastrous model for the middle-class English citizen; moreover, he thought that such a citizen was often threatened by a Calvinist religious doctrine that pulverized his very ability to think critically and be skeptical. Arnold nonetheless had very high hopes for that citizen. He could recognize the profound unintellectuality of the middle class, its religious stupefactions, its commercialism. Yet as Trilling says (and he knew "Ecce, Convertimur ad Gentes" very well), ". . . it is such a class that Arnold undertakes to lead to the light of a new era, not now by an appeal to a higher notion of reason but by a simple appeal to utility and the state of the Empire."[22] This faith, this confidence, and these sturdy assumptions are the deepest part of Arnold. We must understand that they are alien to Trilling.

Perhaps this is so because, as John Henry Raleigh has suggested, Arnold was rightly seen by Trilling as a liberal and, ". . . like most liberals, [Arnold] never came to real grips with the problem of power in government."[23] The liberalism Trilling placed under the hard glare of criticism for the whole of his career finds its first full and substantial representative in the person of Matthew Arnold. Arnold is thus to stand for all aspects, the meritorious as well as the shallow, of liberalism. If Arnold falters, therefore, it is liberalism faltering. "The everlasting question of philosophical politics is how to place power and reason in the same agent, or how to make power reasonable, or how to endow reason with power,"[24] says Trilling. He then proceeds to point out that Arnold could not answer the everlasting question. Looking to Arnold's theory of the State, Trilling says that it does not hold up and that "its failure is the typical liberal failure,"[25] for it seeks to avoid the crudities of power.

This is all quite fair, but how much, one may ask, does Trilling want from Arnold? Does he really want him to be able not only to address the question of power, but also to answer it with specifics? Does he wish him to explore, in practical detail, the means by which a representative liberal of great repute is to accommodate himself to situations involving power? The answer is clearly no. Trilling knows there is little sense in asking such questions of Arnold. He knows that Arnold *must* fail in providing such an accommodation. Arnold is in fact to be admired for so doing, because in failure he can give us something better than practical success. He can set forth a high vision of political life and engagement from which we all may learn. The attractiveness of the vision will beckon us onward. It will engage our best selves, touching upon the myriad aspects of our human and political complexity. It will enliven and magnify our possibilities: "The value of any myth [says Trilling] cannot depend on its demonstrability as a fact, but only on the value of the attitudes it embodies, the further attitudes it engenders and the actions it motivates. In these respects Arnold's myth is still fertile and valuable—and morally inescapable."[26]

Trilling's true test for Arnold, then, involved an assessment of the degree to which Arnold's mind was responsive to historical, cultural, and human complexity. Arnold beautifully passed the test. Belonging, as Raleigh summed it up, to the tradition "that values the personal virtues of intelligence, amenity, tolerance, courage, and modulation and flexibility,"[27] Arnold could be offered as an almost perfect example of that which Stalinism must oppose. For as he provided a myth, he provided something else. He made it possible to see that formulaic and systematic thought can be a grotesque *abuse* of the mind. A myth, then, that enhances human possibility and indulges human complexity versus a political reality, a system, that rigidifies and delimits those same things: the lines are drawn by Trilling in 1939 as neatly and as forcibly as they can be. Or almost. For Trilling himself is nothing if not complex. Arnold does not, in fact, *perfectly* represent the human and cultural potential that is to stand in the way, if anything can, of Stalinism. Arnold is defective—subtly, so. It is not, finally, that he misunderstands power and its application. It is not that he is occasionally vague and inexact. Nor is it that he was likely to confuse "serious" literature with the merely solemn, or that he engaged in his own amateur theories of obnoxious racialism. It is that Arnold is flawed by his optimism. He is flawed by a spontaneity of hope that is, whenever severely put to the test, found to be without substance. Arnold wanted, as Trilling says, to be a liberal not of today, but "of the future."[28] He looked to liberalism as a means by which the instinct of human expansion could be satisfied, but ". . . only to a Liberalism which can perceive and understand *all* the parts and powers of expansion and serve them all."[29] And this liberalism, a culture to oppose anarchy, is not, as Trilling was to make a career of discovering, to be found in the world as it is. The world as it is will not have it. The violent, cruel world of Stalinism, and the shabby, vulgar world of a bloated, absorptive middle class will not have it. A graver, tougher, more skeptical, and more resilient vision must be drawn out of a world damaged, perhaps irreparably, by Stalinism and by mass culture. That, after 1939, would be Trilling's uninviting task. Pursuing it, mindful of what he saw as Arnold's liberal excesses of hope, he would learn to temper and restrain severely his own liberal sentiments.

6. The Lessons of Conservatism and the Lesson of E. M. Forster

AT NO TIME in his career did Lionel Trilling find systems, either aesthetic or political, attractive. For him, the sign of a mind not fully cultivated was, in fact, its yielding to system. Stalinism was one great system, and the most alarming example in his life of what systems could come to mean and to do. Matthew Arnold, on the other hand, had been unsystematic, even if he had been capable of producing arresting metaphorical classifications such as "our society distributes itself into Barbarians, Philistines, and Populace" or "the governing idea of Hellenism is spontaneity of consciousness: that of Hebraism, strictness of conscience." In Trilling's mind, then, Arnold could be made to stand for something wholly unlike Stalinism and the lesser stalinisms of the underdeveloped mind. He could be made also to stand for something unlike the kind of American liberalism that had not protested Stalinism energetically enough. Calling for subtlety, a recognition of differences amid similarities, curiosity, and a constant study of perfection and its elusiveness, Arnold, even an imperfect and unduly optimistic Arnold, could for Trilling exemplify mind not sunk into claustrophobia, rigidity, or willed innocence and befuddlement.

Trilling never expected the example to dominate in his own time. He simply hoped it would have a claim on some of his fellow American intellectuals, those for whom the appropriate word—part pronoun and part praise—was "we." Arnold had written: "I am a Liberal, yet I am a Liberal

tempered by experience, reflection and renouncement. . . ."
Trilling knew how remote the chances were that the liberals
surrounding him could thus be tempered, but Arnold's hope
was his. In the late 1930's and 1940's, however, it was a hope
much darkened by suspicions about the middle-class intellectuals to whom he was speaking. Oddly enough, Arnold's hope
was not unlike that expressed by Marx and Engels when they
envisaged "a small section of the ruling class" cutting itself
adrift, acquiring by directly active means the consciousness
of the proletariat, and thereafter holding the future in its
hands. Arnold had written: ". . . in each class there are born
a certain number of natures with a curiosity about their best
self, with a bent for seeing things as they are, for disentan-
gling themselves from machinery, for simply concerning themselves with reason and the will of God, and doing their best
to make these prevail."[1] Now and again permitting himself
hope, Trilling meditated on Arnold and thought about the
same thing happening in his own time and place. One obvious difference would be that the latter-day Trilling would
not include, in his hope, "the will of God."

Such optimism was only occasional, however, because in
the 1940's he was convinced that the tendencies of contemporary culture were almost wholly destructive. Liberals, to
be sure, were in the ascendant, but liberals could be trusted
only to make the life of the mind less than it might be. In
now reminding ourselves just how caustic Trilling could become in the face of what he saw as the surrender of his own
class of intellectuals, let us refer to what he had to say about
them in 1948 in a symposium on American writing sponsored
by *Partisan Review*:

. . . the mass of educated people—of intellectuals indeed—are
becoming increasingly suspicious of culture and even hostile toward it. They don't know this and certainly they wouldn't admit
it, for culture still has honorific meanings for the middle class.
Yet the fact is that in their hearts they more and more reject the
traditional methods of art. . . .

It is no doubt very easy to say that what I have been describing is simply Philistinism. And it is the easier because certain Philistines have undertaken to speak for this cultural group and to attack high-brow culture as pretentious or irresponsible or corrupt or insane. It is also possible to call it Stalinism, for Stalinism becomes endemic in the American middle class as soon as that class begins to think. . . .[2]

The spirit here is a familiar one in our time. So is the bitterness. Ortega y Gasset shared it. So did T. S. Eliot. Henry Adams had grave doubts about the masses; so did Yeats. Alexander Hamilton had thought the American crowd a "beast"; in England, Carlyle had written splenetically against the same animal-like force. The tradition of conservative thought is rich with such horror and such suspicion. The common reader, a democratic self amid books, is welcomed only when he is alone, never when he approaches as part of a group. Trilling's contribution to such opinion is his belief that the local, and oppressive, version of Philistinism in his time is to be defined by its connections with a certain system of political thought and regimentation. Other anxious commentators have seen the precise opposite: massness is squalid and destructive because of its confusions, its lack of discipline, its refusal to tolerate consistency. Trilling believes otherwise: that it is all too consistent.

Despite his belief that Stalinism was the most significant cultural legacy of the turbulent 1930's, and that its tendency to systematize vulgar thought was its chief danger, Trilling was not happy at all with the form of literary and critical thought proposed in some quarters as the corrective to political and historical reductionism—the New Criticism. Deprived of historical and social context, stripped of everything but the precisions of verbal method, and given over to the successes of pedagogy, the New Criticism seemed to some teachers and writers a perfect means of fleeing the pressures of the recent past. Trilling thought otherwise. He believed that one did not oppose ideology with no ideology, but with a more refined, more capacious, and more supple (that is, Arnoldian) ideology. The New Criticism, moreover, had never left the Academy—or so he argued. It had never entered the world where literature, a central part of culture in its indivisible entirety, was really found. It had not begun to make even the necessary exertions to do so:

It has not made its way among the groups that might be expected to feel its influence. After nearly twenty years of activity, it is still the *new* criticism. . . . [E]ven now, when it has won its way at least in academic circles, quite scaring the old-line scholars into apologetic self-consciousness, it makes out that it is still ·misunderstood. It has mistaken method for ideology, and pretends that all it offers is method. It should long ago have realized and admitted its ideology and carried its ark into battle.[3]

Trilling's aversion to the New Criticism,* on the grounds that it was not only a system, but a system without energy or color, was transformed over time into an aversion to any form of literary and cultural study devoid of historical and political connections. Against latter-day structuralism, phenomenology, aestheticism pure and impure; against forms of psychohistorical understanding lacking a traditional historical awareness; against any uses of the mind that did not embrace what he saw as the essentially *conditioned* nature of worldly existence—Trilling, with circumspection, took his stand, first in one decade, then in another.† He stood against the New Criticism just as Edmund Burke had once stood against the ideologues of the French Revolution. Burke had said: "Cir-

---

*Characteristically enough, Trilling allowed his penchant for the abstract to control his view of the New Critics. He saw them *en bloc*. He mentioned none by name, and apparently refused to see, as well he might have, that the roots of the New Criticism grew in part out of ideology, out of a conservative southern resistance to the modernization of culture along liberal guidelines. Nor did he remark that the best of the New Critics—R. P. Blackmur, John Crowe Ransom, and Allen Tate—possessed the "complexity and variousness" of mind that he himself revered.

†See, for instance, his hostility to what he calls "the infant discipline of psychohistory" in his "Introduction" to the reissue of *The Middle of the Journey* (New York, 1975), p. xxii (originally published in *The New York Review of Books*, XXII, no. 6 [Apr. 17, 1975], pp. 18–24).

cumstances (which with some gentlemen pass for nothing) give in reality to every political principle its distinguishing colour and discriminating effect. The circumstances are what render every civil and political scheme beneficial or noxious to mankind."[4] For the rest of his career, Trilling was to make this lesson from Burke his own.

Trilling's aversion to system made his later preoccupation with Freud unusual. He was never concerned with tracing the elaboration of the Freudian system of analysis and inter-pretation. With the highly specialized neologisms Freud es-tablished to describe areas of psychic activity, with the dis-tinctions employed to demarcate forms of neurosis, with the connections devised to bring an understanding of physiology over into an understanding of mentality—with all these things Trilling was simply not much interested. It is another aspect of Freud, one developed late in his life, that Trilling takes up: Freud not as clinician but as tragic humanist, the author of *Civilization and Its Discontents*, the prophetic stu-dent of humanity's great aspirations and great limitations. He is interested in Freud, in other words, precisely as Freud brings his mind into its most expansive and gloomy registers. Freud thus enters a category of achievement, as far as Trilling is concerned, where Arnold was before admired. It was one from which Stalinism and the abuses of mind it stood for and encouraged would always be excluded.

The connections between Stalinism and liberalism were, at least in the 1940's, apparently easy for Trilling to make. Solicitous of the middle class, and believing, as Arnold be-lieved, that it was the home of liberalism, he nevertheless was deeply troubled by what he saw as the moral collapse of that class. He expressed some of his feelings in the bitter statement quoted earlier that "Stalinism becomes endemic in the Amer-ican middle class as soon as that class begins to think." But not always did Trilling write so caustically. When he did, however, and when he thus came to the furthest extent of his anger and disappointment, he availed himself of an idea well known to conservatives: If thinking was the problem for the middle class, then why not indict thought? Hence, just a few years after positing the connection between the middle class and Stalinism, he harshly wrote: ". . . in general I do not believe that a high incidence of conscious professional intellect in a society necessarily makes for a good future."[5] This deep reservation about thought, about the merits and rewards of thinking, is preserved throughout the rest of his career. We shall see more of it as we go along, but it is only one aspect of a mind that otherwise had the highest aspirations for thought and was capable of confidence in the vast reservoir of possibility surviving in the class he saw as his own.

The strategy governing Trilling's life as a critic in the 1940's and 1950's was, as I have said, to evaluate the "liberal" imagination. Or, as Stephen Spender once put it, the *lack* of a liberal imagination.[6] Trilling, as self-proclaimed liberal, would put liberalism under scrutiny. With procedures everywhere careful, and with the greatest patience, Trilling sought for a number of years to reveal the dichotomy—a stark one, as he saw it—between the admirable sentiments of liberalism in the United States and the embarrassing poverty of liberal thought. He approached American liberalism with the same courtesy that Arnold had employed in the opening sentence of *Culture and Anarchy* when he referred to ". . . that fine speaker and famous Liberal, Mr. Bright." Arnold went patiently on, we know, to annihilate Mr. Bright and everything he stood for. Trilling also knew that it would be the lambent play of the mind, and never the low stroke, that would serve him best as he undertook his own campaign of chastising liberalism.

Trilling did not write the essays in *The Liberal Imagination* with the assumption that he could mount his attack on that imagination by reference to a more solid and reliable conservative tradition. Nowhere in *The Liberal Imagination* does he seem interested in affording himself the support of such a tradition. He writes otherwise. Hence Spender seems to be beside the point when he refers to Trilling's ". . . quite remarkable unawareness of any points of view which seriously challenge liberalism," or when he says that ". . . it is a pity that Mr. Trilling can find nothing to take seriously in the conservatism of W. H. Auden, Ezra Pound, T. S. Eliot, Allen Tate, Robert Lowell, Peter Viereck, and others. . . ."[7] Such a conservatism does, or did, exist. Trilling was aware of it. But he did not want to embrace it, for the very simple reason that he did not wish, at that time in his career, to be considered a conservative. He proclaimed himself a liberal, a liberal of capaciousness and distinction, a liberal upholding the best of liberalism. That he often, in fact, was conservative in both argument and sensibility would have been an imputation he would then have bitterly resisted. Later in his career, as I shall argue, the imputation would be received more warmly, would be seen not as a "charge" but as a kind of praise.

But in the 1950's Trilling sought to criticize liberalism from *within* liberalism. He sought to reveal its inadequacies (many such, by his count) by calling upon its strengths. He and his criticism, both emboldened by the example of Arnold, would be chief among those strengths. But in order to secure a position within liberalism from which to gain a clear perspective on its frailties and attack them, Trilling was forced continually to remove himself first to one edge, and then to another, and at last to the outermost margins of liberalism. The ground beneath him was again and again found to be either weak or worthy of being forfeited. So, bit by bit, he gave up ground over the years until what was left to him was only sentiments residual within the liberal tradition—a sense of expanded mental and moral faculties, a preference for curiosity, a vague encouragement toward the liberation of self from whatever might constrain self. But such residual sentiments do not make a politics. They make only an atmosphere, an ambience, and Trilling survived for years in an environment of liberalism depleted of its ideas and sustained by its style and attitudes. Real politics are made, even if badly

made, by other sentiments and other passions, more pointed
and particular, at times more ideologically precise, than those
that Trilling was left with. In the late 1940's he seems to have
recognized this fact. In the "Editor's Note" to his *Portable
Matthew Arnold* he says that ". . . it is no longer possible to
take seriously *as thought*—whatever we might want to say of
their right feeling—the political utterances of our liberal
weeklies. Things were different in the nineteenth century."[8]
And, at the same time, in an essay on Rebecca West he makes
a similar declaration: ". . . progressivism has no true awareness of the deep instinctual roots of man . . . what awareness
it does have is likely to be a hostile one, and . . . in this respect
it is in full accord with the acquisitive, competitive society it
wishes to revise."[9]

These statements are characteristic of Trilling because they
turn on his sense of emptiness in liberal thought, his appeal
to an earlier historical moment, and his recognition of "the
deep instinctual roots of man." But out of such stuff liberalism is not customarily made. Conservatism is. Trilling, however, not only made a determined effort to integrate such
attitudes into his liberalism but also made it clear in practice
that he had no belief in a viable conservative tradition.
American thinkers traditionally do not; conservative thought,
as thought, has always wanted sustenance in the United States
—the literary examples of Pound, Peter Viereck, Allen Tate,
and Robert Lowell notwithstanding. For Trilling, conservative truths must be recognized, and the conservative sensibility must, in its gravity, be acknowledged. But if liberalism is
thin and mindless, conservatism is even more inadequate. So,
in the essays in *The Liberal Imagination*, Trilling avails himself not of conservative authority but of conservative pessimism. And that is because he believes conservative authority
has had no greater success in establishing a credible system of
politics (about any such system he would at the outset have
had doubts) than has liberal authority. The truths of conserva-

tism, then, have *uses* for Trilling, but they are not superior to the liberal attitudes they oppose.

In having thought earlier (in 1940) about T. S. Eliot—obviously a conservative, and obviously a mind seriously to be reckoned with—Trilling had expressed great admiration. Eliot had once been obliged to confront Arnold's legacy, and the encounter had helped to define his criticism. And in 1940 it was Trilling who knew he could profit from the same encounter with Eliot. That profitable encounter reveals to us one side of Trilling's political stance: the conservative. Another, and opposing, side is revealed when this admiration on Trilling's part gets severely qualified in his speaking of Eliot's "deficiencies," his "cold ignorance," his "fierce Puritanism," and his "confusion of morality with snobbery or conformity."[10] Here Trilling admits his misgivings about the conservative posture. About power, moreover, Eliot knew nothing. One good way of summing up Trilling's ambivalent attitude toward Eliot is John Henry Raleigh's. He says that though Trilling believes "Eliot's whole position is manifestly impractical . . . he should be listened to, as Mill listened to Coleridge."[11] When Mill listened to Coleridge, he had this to say: " 'Lord, enlighten thou our enemies' . . . sharpen their wits, give acuteness to their perceptions and consecutiveness and clearness to their reasoning powers: we are in danger from their folly, not from their wisdom. . . ."[12]

This prayer is often found repeated in Trilling's writings from 1940 on. It was a familiar element in his rhetorical strategies. Trilling saw much folly in conservatism—as much, indeed, as in liberalism. But that he could see so much folly wherever he looked should remind us of how estranged he was from the two political traditions he spent a career interpreting. He stood at the margin of liberalism, keenly aware of the impoverishments of all the connecting territory. He knew enough of conservatism to be aware of its final sterilities. The ventilation of mind involved in the first attracted him; the tonic pessimism of the second sustained him. But a workable synthesis of the two was not easily forthcoming.

The energy behind Trilling's antipathy to American liberalism and progressivism in the 1940's issued only partly from his adoption of conservative attitudes. About those attitudes, as I have said, he had his suspicions. He drew into play, therefore, not political notions but geographical ones to repulse liberalism. He turned away from the nation whose cultural sensibility he felt deficient and looked elsewhere for support. "Since the Renaissance," he wrote, in thinking about E. M. Forster, "and especially in the 18th century, it had been a device of moralists to confront their own culture with the superior habits of foreign lands."[13] In the nineteenth century, Arnold had turned his mind to France—the home of a revolution, a center of order and strength, the site of an Academy, a source of culture. By comparison England seemed to him chaotic and individualistic. Trilling wrote of Arnold's description of the contrast:

England's geniuses had been solitary, individualistic—and discontinuous. Shakespeare may have far surpassed Corneille, Newton had excelled Leibnitz: the Continental instinct for order, however, had compensated for the inferiority in endowed energy.
. . .
The French people, indeed, were preeminent in their understanding of the virtue of submitting the individual genius to law, of subordinating energy to intelligence. The English lacked this perception and in the Romantic period they had been unable to advance beyond a wonderful outburst of energy.[14]

As France thus figured for Arnold as a means of defining his feelings toward England, so England and the Continent figured for Trilling in his examination of America.* "Lib-

*Trilling's liking for things English has been reciprocated by the favorable attention his writings have received in that country. The English, recognizing the strong Arnoldian flavor of his literary sensibility, see him as a critic happily free of American provincialism. They thus assimilate him to their own provincialism.

eralism" for the Trilling of the 1940's was a thoroughly American phenomenon; about its forms elsewhere he had no interest. Moreover, liberalism *was*, for all intents, America. In the famous preface to *The Liberal Imagination*, written in 1949, he had made the equation: "In the United States at this time liberalism is not only the dominant but even the sole intellectual tradition."[15]

To control a perspective, then, from which this dominant tradition may be surveyed, and to do so without entangling oneself with the embarrassments of conservatism (called in 1949 ". . . irritable mental gestures which seek to resemble ideas"),[16] Trilling removes himself from the American intellectual landscape. He moves first to E. M. Forster; he moves away from Theodore Dreiser and John Dos Passos* toward Henry James; he moves away from Karen Horney and Erich Fromm toward the more pessimistic psychoanalytic views of Sigmund Freud; he moves away from V. L. Parrington so that he may read Tacitus; Wordsworth's sense of mortality is employed to illuminate the thin shabbiness of American businessmen; Wordsworth's moral gravity stands as a rebuke to the preciosities of the New Critics; the superficiality of the American novel is revealed at once when it is compared with the European. The distance from which he views the objects he considers gives him a perspective he thought utterly inaccessible to his countrymen. In 1939, in an earlier symposium in *Partisan Review* on the state of American writing, he had seen the direction he was to take: "In my own case, for example, though I have great admiration and affection for the American classics and an increasing interest, I know that they have been far less important to me than the traditional body of European writers."[17]

The study of E. M. Forster that Trilling wrote in 1943 provides the first corrective to things liberal and things Amer-

---

*For Trilling's largely negative appraisal of Dos Passos, in which the comparison is explicitly made with Forster, see "The America of John Dos Passos," *Partisan Review*, IV, no. 5 (Apr. 1938), pp. 26–32.

ican. A short book, it is not so much written as aimed. It carries, gracefully, a certain burden of literary criticism; more importantly, it carries Trilling's digressions on matters only remotely connected to Forster. Such ulterior purposes were fully acknowledged when he introduced its second edition (1964). Looking back, Trilling reported:

> . . . I have no doubt that I was benefited by the special energies that attend a polemical purpose. To some readers it will perhaps seem strange, even perverse, to have involved Mr. Forster in polemic, but I did just that—I had a quarrel with American literature as at that time it was established, and against what seemed to me its dullness and its pious social simplicities I enlisted Mr. Forster's vivacity, complexity, and irony.[18]

Trilling's "quarrel" with American literature and culture went on, as we know, for a good long while. The various subjects embraced by digressions in this book are those he was to write about for years. *E. M. Forster* is the book where he brings together his attitudes on the virtues of moral realism, the "incompetence" of liberalism to deal either with death or with tragedy, the inextricable mixture of good with evil, the liabilities of the energized intellect, and the attractiveness of the human will in its relaxed state. To each of these matters Forster is made to lend his own odd conservative sensibility. He does so, as Trilling is pleased to point out, in a wholly "non-lugubrious" way; as a writer, Forster makes his way by virtue of an "implacable gentleness."[19] He does not, in other words, have the American problem: he is serious when necessary, but he never sees the merit of being solemn.

Moreover, with his surprises of plot, his melodrama, his gaiety, his refusal to force issues, his refusal to be "great," even his lack of intellectual perseverance, Forster represents an approach to the strange spectacle of life that Americans would be expected to find too buoyant. In thinking about the frequent occurrence of sudden death in Forster, Trilling remarks on ". . . the brusque casualness, the lack of 'reason' and 'motivation' which invariably marks his deaths."

One thing to say is that certain kinds of unmotivated events in fiction represent what happens in life. Life is not only a matter of logic and motivation but of chance. . . . In Forster's world death gives a peculiar emphasis to life and it is the essence of the drama of death that it so often is crassly casual.[20]

To liberals, such dealings with death might appear wholly unreasonable. Liberals arrange things so as always to be affronted by the vicissitudes fundamental to existence. Forster (and Trilling after him) sees liberalism, therefore, as incompetent, no matter how sweet its attractions, in the face of tragedy, in the face of death.*

We have seen, in an earlier chapter, just how incapable the "liberal" characters of Trilling's fiction are of coming to terms with death. Here, in Forster, Trilling finds a superb novelist aware of the same liberal inadequacy, and of what it implies. The most desperate weakness of liberalism is the narrowness of its imagination. It can see neither the truly sobering nor the delightfully inconsequential; hence it ". . . is always being surprised. There is always the liberal work to do over again because disillusionment and fatigue follow hard upon surprise, and reaction is always ready for that moment of liberal disillusionment and fatigue—reaction never hopes, despairs or suffers amazement."[21] Liberalism, moreover, is avid for a moral logic by which the good and the bad can be precisely categorized. It cannot understand what Milton

---

*One of the few American writers on whom Trilling in his period could look with favor was Walt Whitman. Whitman is to be valued, he said in 1945, because he was, as a postwar poet, exceptionally sensitive to both the "yes" and the "no" of his culture. He lived amid dualisms and was dialectical in his imagination. He understood that literature is intimately and ineluctably united with politics. And, most importantly, he understood that genuine personal identity grows out of a knowledge of life's proximity to death. Thus Whitman is like Forster in spirit, and Trilling says that the real Whitman is the poet of "Out of the Cradle Endlessly Rocking." In arguing that Whitman believed that ". . . the coming American poets must have a deep consciousness of death," Trilling is of course hearing in Whitman what we hear always in Trilling himself: that death is not to be left out of the accounting, either of literature or of politics. See "Sermon on a Text from Whitman," *Nation* (Feb. 24, 1945), pp. 215–16.

meant when he said that "Good and evil we know in the field of this world grow up together inseparably." "Good-and-evil," the two inseparable, is a paradox beyond liberalism. Yet it is, as far as Forster and Trilling can see, at the very heart of things.

All of this is to say that Forster—unlike countless progressive American novelists of the stripe of Steinbeck or Dreiser, or critics of the stripe of Parrington or Van Wyck Brooks—is a moral realist. For Trilling this is not merely a description. It is the highest sort of praise. Being a moral realist involves one, moreover, in historical understanding. One is not surprised, or embarrassed, or left alone as a moral realist. One travels with a sense of history in one's bones. "Forster knows, as [Sherwood] Anderson never knew, that things are really there," says Trilling.[22] They are there because the past has left them around. They should please us by virtue of their odd circumstantiality.

As a moral realist, as one ". . . content with the human possibility and content with its limitations,"[23] Forster, according to Trilling, has the most cautious attitudes toward the human intellect. To put it more simply: the Forster Trilling admires distrusts the mind. Trilling shares that distrust. The human intellect is seen as the very thing that can disorient moral realism. In its rigidities, in its ferociousness, in "the everlasting research of the mind into itself," intellect is dangerous. It is the force that the young Matthew Arnold, for instance, once was obliged to repel in order to live. It is, for Forster, a "treacherous" force when it reaches certain intensities. For Arnold, for Forster, and for Trilling, intellect exists in opposition to "the life of acceptant calm" or "the life of simple instinct." As a rarefied power, intellect can do nothing but harm. Trilling sees Forster as one who eschewed intellect and turned to something else—which in this book is praised as the "strange virtue of weariness." One learns, if one attains to wisdom, to be passive; one learns how best to be defeated. As Forster said in 1941: "To me the best chance for

future society lies through apathy, uninventiveness and inertia."[24] The fervent powers of will, inspiring intellect, must be
renounced, for Forster's work ". . . speaks to us of a world
where the will is not everything and it suggests that where
the will is not everything it will be a better and a more effective will."[25]

This animus against will is fundamental in Trilling's development as a moral critic. The example of Forster, come to
as a subject during wartime, supplies him with assumptions
and attitudes that he is to exploit as long as he writes. His
attitude toward Forster in the 1940's draws him, moreover,
into a most curious moment of historical analysis. The treacherous and intense evolution of the intellect, says Trilling, has
been accompanied by an expansion of the will in all its excesses. Where once we might have learned wisdom in passivity and inertia, we are now conditioned to prize intellect
made ever more active. The roots of this situation lie in the
French Revolution and in the fervent anti-religiosity of the
eighteenth century. The small lawyers and small priests in
the Assembly, men unprepared for state management, were
correctly seen by Edmund Burke as dangerous to the proper
workings of government, first in France and later elsewhere.
Trilling also echoes Burke in saying that the intellectual *qua*
intellectual was also a product of the French Revolution,
which ". . . was the first great occasion when Mind—conscious, verbalized mind—became an important element in
national politics."[26] Added to Mind was a "moral and pious
aspect," which derived from the breakup of many passionate
religious orthodoxies. Strong religious feelings were, in the
eighteenth century, transferred to secular life. The result was
that many intellectuals, newly sprung into life, were endowed
with ". . . the sense of morality, the large feelings and the intellectual energy that had once been given to religion."[27]

The long-term effects of this historical process, Trilling
feels, have been nothing but dismaying. Bathed in what he

terms "an aura of self-congratulation," the intellectual has now become smug, intoxicated with his own sense of good will, and oblivious to the fact that ". . . the love of humanity has its own vices and the love of truth its own insensibilities."[28] Moreover, the intellectual establishes divisions between himself and others. Believing himself the freest of all men, he is actually the most class-bound; believing himself beyond prejudice, he is everywhere hampered by prejudice. Owing to the hyperdevelopment of his powers of articulation, he cannot talk to others of his own class, the middle class. More separated from other people, of all classes, than he is ever prepared to understand, he nevertheless regards all other people as, Trilling says, "objects of his benevolence." Is he not superior to them—"paternal, pedagogic, even priestlike"?[29]

Thus, in 1943, runs Trilling's brief history of the intellectual, and of his terrible shortcomings, since his unfortunate birth during the frenzies of 1789. It is a strange history for a number of reasons, chief among them the unrelieved concentration on the baleful aspects of intellectual development to the exclusion of all other aspects. The reader is therefore left with the sense of a wholly disruptive entity—intellect— thrust suddenly upon the world with will alone to guide it. The odd thing, however, is that Trilling was not always so doleful in his writing of history. In fact, three years before the appearance of *E. M. Forster* he had said:

The French Revolution was advanced on the warmest considerations of personality—one thinks of Montaigne's Montaigne, of Rousseau's Rousseau and his Emile, of Diderot's d'Alembert and his Rameau's nephew. And it is incidentally significant that, after this time, in every nation touched by the Revolution, the novel should have taken on its intense life. For what so animated the novel of the nineteenth century was the passionate—the "revolutionary"—interest in what man should be. It was, that is, a moral interest, and the world had the sense of a future moral revolution.[30]

Thus Trilling in 1940. It is not the same as Trilling in 1943. In the earlier accounting he draws a wholly different picture of the forces liberated by 1789. In the earlier reading of history, Trilling sees personality enhanced, morality enlarged, man himself writ larger, and the novel—a central medium expressive of middle-class aspirations—enlivened. John Henry Raleigh was only partially correct when he said that "a man is known by the tradition in which he sees himself, and Trilling's tradition is in the line of Arnold, the Romantics, and the ideology of the French Revolution."[31] We see that for Trilling the history inaugurated by the Revolution is at one time considered a bright progress and at a later time a journey into chaos. In the course of Trilling's career the latter reading, I believe, gains ascendancy. As time goes on, it becomes clearer and clearer to him that will and intellect, liberated, have become dangerous. The long-term cause of such a deterioration is, he believes, the advent of Marxist psychology. Marx claimed to have a "science" of society and employed, Trilling says, ". . . a concept of materialistic and dialectical causation."[32] In the end, this made obsolete any notions of human morality and human dignity. True corruption thus entered the course of history when one powerful yet inadequate ideology—Marxism—supplanted its own nobler antecedents. What took over was ". . . a view of man shared alike by Liberal manufacturing Whig and radical philosopher, the view that man was very simple and individually of small worth in the cosmic or political scheme."[33] Wordsworth had left the Revolution because, early on, he had come to the same understanding of the corruption that is now Trilling's understanding. In 1943, the immediate cause of such a darkened vision on Trilling's part, and of such a changed reading of history, was his apprehension that ". . . a world at war is necessarily a world of will."[34] Once the Second World War ended, however, another war, a war of will and minds, began. And that war, the Cold War, never truly ceased, as far as Trilling could see, in his lifetime. During that war intellect and will were encouraged to prosper. Intellect and will never retreated. Intellect grew more imperial; will never relaxed. The deadly reductiveness of Marxism was steadily on the march. Trilling always wanted the positive aspects, as he sometimes saw them, of the French Revolution to win out. But he believed that they would not, that they would be overwhelmed by the negative aspects, the infections of mind driven to extremes.

7. The Liberal Imagination and the Lack of Liberal Imagination

E. M. Forster celebrates, quietly, the negative capabilities upon whose unlikely yet great strengths artists may learn to rely. If the will is attenuated, if intellect grows less imperious, then the beneficial oddness of art may prosper. The genuine artist must cease making claims outward on existence. He must allow himself to be claimed. If the exterior world of public events is one of war or threat of war, if exacerbated passion is the rule of the day, then art will be best by being still. Otherwise the voice of the artist will be lost in the great public noise. In the wartime Forster book, Trilling thus calls attention to a sensibility that is almost unattainable but overwhelmingly attractive. It can, he hopes, overcome the insensate life surrounding it. It can discover open places in situations otherwise sealed up and can define subtleties of experience otherwise lost to view. By indirection and passivity it can make richer one's sense of life.

The Liberal Imagination (1950), attentive to the same problems, proposes wholly different answers. As a collection of essays and addresses originally published between 1940 and 1949, it reflects both Trilling's sense of wartime anxieties and his sense of how the end of war was to continue politics by other means. As is customary with Trilling, he only rarely specifies surrounding political circumstances; but there can be no doubt that he was distressed by them. Particularly in the years immediately following the war, he seems alert to the new pressures intellectual life would have to bear. As he says in his 1948 essay on *The Princess Casamassima*, the war had taught everyone ". . . what very few people wish to admit, that civilization has a price, and a high one" (p. 80).* Elsewhere in the book, he remarks morosely on "our grim, late human present" ("Art and Neurosis," p. 175) and informs his readers that ". . . our fate, for better or worse, is political" ("The Function of the Little Magazine," p. 96). Rightly seen today as a critic without a sharp sense of local historical circumstances and with a circumlocutory style and circumspect mind that kept him always at a distance from brute reality, Trilling seems in 1947, in "Manners, Morals, and the Novel," oddly prescient: "It is probable that at this time we are about to make great changes in our social system. The world is ripe for such changes and if they are not made in the direction of greater social liberality, the direction forward, they will almost of necessity be made in the direction backward, of a terrible social niggardliness" (p. 214).

The Liberal Imagination, insofar as it directly confronts historical circumstances, is clearly a postwar book. More than half of its extraordinary, and extraordinarily influential, essays were published after the war, an event that had simply erased, from the large intellectual community for which Trilling felt a responsibility to speak, its vocabulary of conventional political responses.† The American Marxist radicals had seen their ranks thinned even before 1939: the Moscow trials, and the "experimental" war in Spain, followed as they

---

*All page references to *The Liberal Imagination* are to the 1953 Anchor Books edition.

†Writing in 1948 on Rebecca West (in an essay not collected in *The Liberal Imagination*), Trilling says that his readers might be ". . . the very people who a decade ago would have dealt with the idea of the nation not quite as a superstition but as, at best, a primitive survival. . . ." He says that they are now ". . . ready to listen, if not yet to agree, as Miss West speaks of the nation as one of the primary facts of social life." See "Treason in the Modern World," *Nation* (Jan. 10, 1948), p. 46. The old virtue of patriotism did not now seem, to Trilling, homely at all, and he wanted to advertise its attractions to his readers.

were by the Nazi-Soviet pact, had had a devastatingly depress-
ing effect on formal Stalinist connections. The movement in
the United States was either away from politics altogether, or
to a form of Marxist opposition like Trotskyism. The editors
of the influential *Partisan Review* did not cease being political, but they sought to unite a strong concern with the arts
and a strong interest in the Trotskyist alternative. After the
war, such prestigious "front" organizations as the League of
American Writers could not easily be reestablished. Their
momentum had been lost. After all, only Dwight Macdonald
and a few other intellectuals had been able to maintain, in
public print, a doctrine of passive resistance to the war while
it was being pursued: the young Robert Lowell, for his part,
had sat it out, some of the time in the West Street Jail, as a
conscientious objector. But for most Americans, it had been
a moral struggle without ambiguity. The enemy was the
enemy; one's friends were one's friends; in the struggle
against Hitler virtue resided in that friendship.

Hence, for many American intellectuals, doctrinaire leftism of the old Stalinist sort seemed impossible after 1945. But
a sentimental regard for the Soviet Union was not out of the
question. Among certain "fellow travelers," some of whom
rallied to the presidential campaign of Henry Wallace in
1948, "the dominant attitude," as David Caute has said, "was
one of guilt and a sense of gratitude to Russia for her immense sacrifices."[1] For such people, the new source of international difficulty was the West in general and the foreign
policy of the United States in particular. They argued that
the United States had willfully broken up the alliance with
the Soviet Union and was now embarked upon a program of
expansion designed to promote its interests against those
rightfully claimed by its former friend.* For Trilling, how-

---

*This line of thought and version of history lost strength in the 1950's but
regained a considerable amount of it in the late 1960's. For such "revisionist"
historical interpretations, see the works of William Appleman Williams,

ever, this new antagonism, whatever its substance, simply did not achieve the dignity of genuine thought. The leftists who were talking it up, were, as usual, hopelessly muddled. There was nothing of intellectual interest in their arguments about the Cold War. Those arguments were but another example of the way in which circumstances, events, and particularities could act to deaden the American liberal mind. Trilling was attentive to those clotted circumstances, and he wanted to move somewhere beyond them. In 1948, in the essay "Art and Fortune," he said: "But now there is no conservative tradition and no radical tradition of political thought, and not even an eclecticism which is in the slightest degree touched by the imagination; we are in the hands of the commentator" (p. 254).

His sentiments are similar to those of Robert Lowell, who greeted the inauguration of Eisenhower, and the era of clichés and somnambulism it preceded, with the phrase "cyclonic zero of the word." Trilling believed then that "we are in the full time of those desperate perceptions of our life . . ." (p. 257), but he also believed that genuine thought and imagination were withering all around him. Among those desperate perceptions was one he might well have shared with Harold Rosenberg: that the Cold War was itself an intellectually bankrupt phenomenon. Examining it for *Partisan Review* in 1962, Rosenberg wrote: "The cold war is the product of people who are neither radicals nor conservatives and who therefore feel threatened by every revolutionary event, to which their own limits have contributed. Today, both East and West are run by "liberals" who would like to serve the ideal of freedom, on one side, and that of socialism, on the other."[2]

In *The Liberal Imagination*, then, Trilling takes up his contentions against the intellectual conventionalities of his

David Horowitz, Gabriel Kolko, and, for a particularly coarse and tendentious example, the introduction by Garry Wills to Lillian Hellman's *Scoundrel Time* (Boston, 1977). Ms. Hellman was a most ardent Wallace supporter and a most active apologist for the conduct of the Soviet Union after the war.

society. In the 1940's and 1950's he believed, as did Harold
Rosenberg later, that the chief reality offered by the Cold
War was that of a stultifying conformity. *The Liberal Imagination*, his most influential and his most contentious book,
asks not for the negative capabilities of the mind, or for a
reduction of the will, but for the will once again to appear,
now newly defined: "Surely the great work of our time is the
restoration and reconstitution of the will" (p. 258). Writing
thus in 1948, in the "Art and Fortune" essay, Trilling must
have been well aware that five years earlier he had protested
the excesses of the will and had warned that the world might
be treated first to paroxysms of unobstructed will and then
to a ". . . panic and emptiness which make their onset when
the will is tired from its own excess."[3] By 1948, he certainly
had not changed his mind about those excesses: ". . . the will
of our society is dying of its own excess. The religious will,
the political will, the sexual will, the artistic will—each is dying of its own excess" (p. 258). If anything, the situation had
worsened. But against this deterioration of intellectual life,
Trilling offered another force. He offered art. Later in his
career he would not be so confident in such an offering—for
art was later to disappoint—but now art, or more precisely
the classic novel, was chosen to stand against the profanities
of the will. The novel at its best had never rejected will; it
had absorbed it, made it its central concern, celebrated its
most magnificent employments. It had explored the will of
"the young man from the provinces," Julien Sorel and all his
counterparts, who would someday triumphantly enter "the
fair courts of life." And it had seen how true heroism can
come, as it came at last to Sorel, when the will had ". . . exhausted all that part of itself which naturally turns to the inferior objects offered by the social world" and when it had
then ". . . learned to exist in the strength of its own knowledge
of its thought and desire" (Art and Fortune," p. 259). It had
studied, and had devastatingly criticized, the inferior will of
the aspiring middle classes. It had taken the measure of their

ambition and had, in its own large vision, rebuked it. In *The Liberal Imagination* Trilling gives his highest praise to the great realistic novels of the nineteenth century. He praises them as Arnold might have praised them, for being a literary form fully open to the variousness of life. In so doing, he touches upon one thesis of his book:

The novel has had a long dream of virtue in which the will, while never abating its strength and activity, learns to refuse to exercise itself upon the unworthy objects with which the social world tempts it, and either conceives its own right objects or becomes content with its own sense of its potential force—which is why so many novels give us, before their end, some representation, often crude enough, of the will unbroken but in stasis. ("Art and Fortune," p. 260.)

Against this form of noble will stands another: the modern will. These two represent the "yes" and the "no" of the surrounding culture. The modern will now seems to Trilling the stronger, but that is the result of its success in stripping away the constraints and limitations imposed by the specific situations in which it is found. It seeks *pure* manifestations; it is ". . . the will that hates itself and finds its manifestations guilty and is able to exist only if it operates in the name of virtue, that despises the variety and modulations of the human story and longs for an absolute humanity, which is but another way of saying a nothingness" ("The Princess Casamassima," p. 88).

The noble will, on the other hand, depicted in its complex fullness in the great nineteenth-century novels, refuses, as Trilling says, to exercise itself in an unworthy fashion. It rejects anything that gives short shrift to the complications so fundamentally a part of life, anything that denies the dialectical nature of social existence, anything that makes uniform the various.

The Liberal Imagination is in part concerned with examining some of these unworthy phenomena. Trilling has an elementary way of putting this distinction between forms of will; it comes in his well-known 1946 comparison of Henry

James and Theodore Dreiser. "With that juxtaposition," he
says in "Reality in America," "we are immediately at the dark
and bloody crossroads where literature and politics meet" (p.
8). James represents the will fully conditioned to respond to
every motion, no matter how minute or contrary, of the human mind and the social passions. Dreiser represents the will
in its grossest reductions. Rooted in material reality, the inferior imagination of Dreiser shies away from mind and leads
his American readers where they will always naturally go:
toward a kind of heavy-lidded response to the obvious:
". . . with us it is always a little too late for mind, yet never
too late for honest stupidity; always a little too late for understanding, never too late for righteous, bewildered wrath; always too late for thought, never too late for naïve moralizing"
(p. 16).

This powerful, in fact rancorous, passage is familiar to all
of Trilling's readers. A less familiar version came in 1942
when, in "The Sense of the Past," he praised a full sense of
the historical past and observed that "Karl Marx, for whom
history was indeed a sixth sense, expressed what has come to
be the secret hope of our time, that man's life in politics,
which is to say, man's life in history, shall come to an end"
(p. 190).* Trilling has in mind in this essay the apocalyptic
Marx, the prophet who could envision ways in which the
"nightmare" of history in all of its turbulent confusions
might somehow be terminated. He associates this Marx with
modern-day progressives, whose trust in the "onward march"
of time leads them to believe in the coming of a society, just
and harmonious, that "shall be satisfactory once and for all,
time without end" (p. 190). With the liberals, whose strangely
nihilistic beliefs are among the "unworthy objects" with

---

*In 1962, writing on "The Leavis-Snow Controversy" in *Beyond Culture*,
Trilling put the same thought in only slightly different language. He referred
to ". . . the temper of intellectuals today—we all want politics not to exist,
we all want that statement of Hegel's to be absolutely and immediately true,
we dream of reason taking over the whole management of the world, and
soon." See Chapter 9 below.

which the social world tempts the contemporary mind, Marx shares the notion that the burden of history can be lifted by an exercise of the will.

If Trilling's opposition of James and Dreiser may now seem too easy, his opposition of Marx and Freud may not. It is the latter, of course, whom Trilling favors and is to favor all his life. Freud illuminates where no other light shines. As Trilling said of him in 1945: ". . . he ultimately did more for our understanding of art than any other writer since Aristotle" ("Art and Neurosis," p. 156). Even with his regrettable lapses into system-building, his shallow interpretation of Shakespeare,* and his "very conception of art" (which Trilling terms "inadequate" [p. 43]), Freud nonetheless emerges as *the* figure of consequence if one wishes to speak sensibly of that special human engagement with reality called art. Marx, who seems to promise so much, and who seems innocent of the sort of miscalculations or errors to which Freud was liable, proves useless at last. Marx recognized many truths, but not the final truth. To his credit, he did see that the form of culture is struggle, and is nothing if not a dialectic. He did see that a true reading of a culture must be attentive to both the "yes" and the "no" within it. And he taught a lesson that Americans would always willfully ignore: that reality is hard, material, and substantial, and that it cannot be shed by an escape into abstractions. Yet all this is not enough. Marx fails because he is obtuse to the central reckoning, in any developed culture, between human sensibility and irreducible human fact. The great artist stands somewhere within that reckoning, giving life to the sensibility and wishing always to respect the human fact while yet transforming it. Marx, in a word, is oblivious to imagination.† Freud, on the other hand, gives

---

*Trilling says that Freud's "Three Caskets" reading of *King Lear* is not the meaning of that play, ". . . any more than the Oedipus motive is *the* meaning of *Hamlet*" ("Freud and Literature," p. 46). And he belittles the Ernest Jones reading of *Hamlet*, derived as it is from Freudian theory.

†"The life of man, we are now willing to believe, is much more complex and more obscurely rooted than any merely economic investigation will dis-

us a way of thinking ". . . which makes poetry indigenous to the very constitution of the mind" ("Freud and Literature," p. 19).

Bogged down in any number of errors resulting from his itch to systematize, the Freud whom Trilling praises in the essays in the 1940's is nevertheless great by virtue of his forays into the wholly unsystematic. What Trilling means when he looks at this parodoxical Freud is that he was at once systematic and unsystematic, attuned to both the Romantic sensibility and the rational positivism of the Enlightenment. His materialism is "simple," says Trilling, as simple as his determinism, and his epistemology is "rather limited" (p. 39). He was a scientist who resisted conceptualism, and he stood against metaphysics. And yet his principles—classic, tragic, and realistic—open the world to the artist, and make it for him more richly complicated. The paradox can be explained when Trilling says we must be prepared to look far beyond the creaky Freudian machinery to see what it has unearthed: ". . . the unconscious mind works without the syntactical conjunctions which are logic's essence. It recognizes no *because*, no *therefore*, no *but*; such ideas as similarity, agreement, and community are expressed in dreams imagistically by compressing the elements into a unity" (p. 50).

Mind so conceived—freed of the formulae, some of them simplistic, that work to imprison it through definition, and aware of things that it alone can produce—this is the legacy of Freud. Trilling is alert early on in this essay to the fact that his reading puts Freud among the Romantics, and he will "give" Freud to the Romantics—only later to take him back. Together the Romantics and Freud do make use of strengths and freedoms arising from their nonrational conception of existence, Trilling says. Poets such as Wordsworth, Coleridge,

---

close." Thus Trilling in "Treason in the Modern World" (p. 48). His reading recognizes in Marx neither a psychology nor a philosophy. Trilling's Marx is the political propagandist, not the author of *The Economic and Philosophic Manuscripts* of 1844 or of *The German Ideology*.

and Arnold discover that "the mind has become far less simple," but also that ". . . this new power may be conspired
against by other agencies of the mind." This struggle, of mind
against itself, of mind responsive to ". . . the hidden element
of human nature and of the opposition between the hidden
and the visible" (p. 34), is to Trilling a vastly more dramatic
and enlivening spectacle than· the bloody struggle of class
against class prophesied by Marx. From what Trilling could
see, the Marxists would give to mind an artificiality foolishly
inappropriate to it. They would "contrive" a mind already
brought to a state of preparedness, already informed by structures of understanding and cognition—a mind, in short,
ready to think. Freud and Trilling would place mind elsewhere, beyond or beneath ratiocination. Responsive only intermittently to the call of reason, this mind can exercise itself
in ways both creative and destructive. Freud's function as a
physician was to assist in the control of the destructive aspect;
as Trilling says, there is an aspect of Freud that recognized
the great responsibility ". . . to strengthen the ego, to make it
more independent of the super-ego, to widen its field of vision, and so extend the organization of the id" (p. 38). The
nightside of life must be discovered. The irrational and the
nonlogical must, for the sake of health, be exposed and
known: "Where id was, there ego shall be." But this Freud,
the rationally constructive, therapeutic Freud, is actually of
minor interest to Trilling. Another Freud, the one wholly
indisposed to any notions of simple humanitarian optimism,
is the Freud he reveres. It is not the romantic Freud, nor the
scientific one. It is the tragic Freud.

With this Freud in mind, Trilling confronts the American
liberals surrounding him and—as he believes—dominating
his culture. The charge against them in *The Liberal Imagination* is straightforward. And by indicting them in this, his
most polemical book, he goes as far as he will ever go in giving a definition to "liberalism." (Those dissatisfied with his
kind of definition must, whatever else they do, see that it is

as precise as Trilling was ever able to make things.) His definition declares that liberals have given themselves a sense of
reality which admits of "neither imagination nor mind."
They endorse the good things: they have, as he says in 1946
in "The Function of the Little Magazine," ". . . a ready if
mild suspiciousness of the profit motive, a belief in progress,
science, social legislation, planning, and international coop-
eration, perhaps especially where Russia is in question" (p.
94). But these admirable sympathies do them no real good
insofar as Trilling is concerned. Their eager charitableness
only reveals their distance from the more exacting and deeper
imaginative culture of their time. Willing their society to be
something it is not, and perpetually disheartened as it proves
unresponsive to their aspirations, the liberals whom Trilling
has in mind err in ways that Freud had foreseen:

When we justly find fault with the present state of our civilization for so inadequately fulfilling our demands for a plan of life
that shall make us happy, and for allowing the existence of so
much suffering which could probably be avoided—when, with
unsparing criticism, we try to uncover the roots of its imperfec-
tion, we are undoubtedly exercising a proper right and are not
showing ourselves enemies of civilization. We may expect gradually to carry through such alterations in our civilization as will
better satisfy our needs and will escape our criticisms. But perhaps we may also familiarize ourselves with the idea that there
are difficulties attaching to the nature of civilization which will
not yield to any attempt at reform.[4]

Thus Freud in 1930 in *Civilization and Its Discontents*. There
are some things the will to reform cannot dislodge. Not to
recognize them is not to recognize what of human striving is
tragic.

The result of liberal misconception is, says Trilling, liberal
deprivation. By their social sympathies, liberals are estranged
from the most important literary achievements of their time.
Trilling's description of this situation in *The Liberal Imagination* has become one of the best-known things about him.
It comes in the "Little Magazine" essay, which he had orig-

inally written as the introduction to an anthology of *Partisan Review* selections from the years 1934–44.

... if ... we name those writers who, by the general consent of the most serious criticism, by consent too of the very class of educated people of which we speak, are to be thought of as the monumental figures of our time, we see that to these writers the liberal ideology has been at best a matter of indifference. Proust, Joyce, Lawrence, Eliot, Yeats, Mann (in his creative work), Kafka, Rilke, Gide—all have their own love of justice and the good life, but in not one of them does it take the form of a love of the ideas and emotions which liberal democracy, as known by our educated class, has declared respectable (p. 94).

This is a powerful and sobering assessment. It owes its memorability to the way Trilling makes the reader see the starkest kind of dichotomy between two great abstractions: "liberal ideology" and "monumental" creativity. And the reader witnesses this dramatic conflict in the presence of someone who speaks with absolute proprietary conviction of "we," of "the very class of educated people," and of "our educated class." The reader is thus made to understand that he is not being treated to mere opinion. He is being given corporate understanding. He is reading a "public" intellectual. Stephen Spender was surely right, however, when he objected in a 1950 review of *The Liberal Imagination* to the starkness with which Trilling had portrayed the situation. Spender said then that it was fallacious for Trilling to argue ". . . that because the best writers are not liberals therefore the liberals have no connection with their work."[5] The fact is that "the alienation" or "the breach" between the educated class for which Trilling elected during his career to act as spokesman and "the deep places of the imagination" is not absolute. Liberals do have a connection with those places, just as Trilling, a liberal shaped by his nonliberal dispensations, does. The real situation is not the one Trilling describes, but one in which liberals feel uneasy, and at times desperately disoriented, when made to confront those "unreformable" aspects of the human endeavor that Freud had once before inspected and that modern writers now explore. Great writers have never avoided such aspects. And liberals, though not ignorant of them, move warily in their presence. That is Trilling's real subject: the limits and inadequacies of liberalism as it is displayed in the United States, not the total failure of liberalism.

Faced with the problem as he sees it so dramatically in the mid-1940's, Trilling proposes his solution. For all his censuring of liberals, and for all his dissatisfaction with their shallow optimism, his solution is in happy accord with the liberal imagination: if there is a breach, why not close it? If there is a spirit of alienation, why not attempt to dissolve it? With a kind of residual Arnoldian spirit spurring him on, he proclaims that ". . . in all our cultural purview there is no work more necessary" than ". . . to organize a new union between our political ideas and our imagination" (pp. 95–96). The steps to be taken must, of course, differ from those taken in the past. If one wishes to bring political ideas and imagination into alignment, one can no longer be tolerant of lesser writing, less serious and less difficult writing. The 1930's, with their proletarian literature, had tried that kind of tolerance and had wound up producing a vastly inferior, now wholly unread and specious art. One must be very solicitous indeed with respect to serious and difficult writing. It is not the element in the equation to be altered. Politics itself must be changed. With a kind of somber optimism at odds with the profoundly conservative spirit he finds so congenial in Freud, Trilling proposes that we conceive of politics differently. He attempts the reconciliation his career had for years been preparing him to make—between the moral life of society and the inner life of individual development, that is, between Arnold and Freud—and this is the way he puts it:

. . . our fate, for better or worse, is political. It is therefore not a happy fate, even if it has an heroic sound, but there is no escape from it, and the only possibility of enduring it is to force into our definition of politics every human activity and every subtlety of every human activity. There are manifest dangers in doing this, but greater dangers in not doing it. Unless we insist that politics is imagination and mind, we will learn that imagination and mind are politics, and of a kind that we will not like (p. 96).

The public consciousness and the private unconsciousness are to be synthesized. One is to be a citizen, and one is to be as aware as possible of oneself. This, then, is how will, "restored and reconstituted," is to be brought into service—or so Trilling says. It is to be given over to redefining politics. And it is to be supervised by the sort of refined and higher liberalism for which, in the late 1940's, Trilling makes himself the optimistically Arnoldian proponent. Hence R. W. B. Lewis was incorrect when, in his review of *The Liberal Imagination*, he hit upon the idea of Trilling as a "contemporary Stoic" and said that *The Liberal Imagination* is no more than ". . . a plan for holding one's own . . . containing the enemy, in the cold war it believes to be always with us." [6] That the Cold War was then on Trilling's mind is beyond question. But Trilling did not, as a result, propose stoicism; he proposed action of his own in the presence of the Cold War. He proposed that ". . . the activity of politics be united with the imagination under the aspect of mind." The agent was to be the will. Let us remind ourselves here again of how differently will had been seen in 1943, when Trilling wrote on Forster.

But it is the single weakness in *The Liberal Imagination*, otherwise a volume so extraordinarily intelligent and provocative, that Trilling nowhere reveals how will is to effect this union. That is perhaps because the necessary outcome of his strategies is, as we shall see, profoundly conservative. And it is because Trilling then resisted the destination toward which his words and attitudes were gradually taking him. To understand his dilemma clearly, let us recount the assumptions underlying *The Liberal Imagination*: literature is not to be denigrated; it is to be seen in its full complexity. Its

variousness lies subtly at the heart of its being. The aspects of
the human condition that are recalcitrant to the simple-
minded impulse to "reform" must be seen for what they are
and respected. They are, after all, central to the life captured
by great literature. All of this is to be carried on with Arnoldian confidence that the social results will be favorable for all
concerned. We will find for ourselves a more capacious, less
ideologically rigid, political sense. Politics will be richer and
less "smelly" as orthodoxies because they will have been saturated by imagination.

So far, so good. The formula is not, however, problem-free.
If politics are to be redefined in order to absorb the more
sinister reaches of the "imagination and mind," they will be
a conservative politics, no matter how strongly Trilling might
wish otherwise. For "imagination and mind," when fully
summoned up, bring both the good and the bad with them.
Imagination invites a malign Iago, as well as a Horatio, into
our consideration. Liberalism is never ready for Iago, but
conservatism anticipates his coming. Liberalism simply could
not then absorb, nor can it now absorb, the destructive de-
mons of modernity surrounding it.

That was a real source of worry for Trilling, real in 1946,
and more real and "exigent" as time went on. It is represented in his phrase "imagination and mind are politics." By
that phrase he means two things: first, that a politics which
omits imagination and mind is a stunted politics; second, that
the dark forces examined by the imagination of modern
writers could be loosed and become murderous in the public
arena. He fears, that is, Nietzsche somehow becoming Hitler,
or the great slumbering Yeatsian beast really slouching into
our newspapers and history. Against such a danger, he proposes that we enlarge our definition of politics to embrace the
beast and Nietzsche as well. But this is no protection against
such things, dislike them though we may. How are we to live
with the undomesticated beast, even though armed with

new definitions? No answer is disclosed. No answer seems possible. Trilling's enlightened modern liberalism, aspiring to do its best, is really no more than wonderful wordplay.

Obviously he then wanted, as almost every modern critic has wanted before and since, a way to read the literature he wanted to read without the contaminations of alien influences. He did not want a shallow politics to constrain a great literature, but he could not locate a suitably deep and "complicated" liberal politics to conjoin with that literature. Conservative politics, a politics that assumed the existence of dark human malignancies, could, of course, sit well with the bitterness of much modern literature, but not with Trilling's professions of a higher liberalism. One escape from the dilemma presented to him would have been a skepticism about the value of that modern literature. The equation *could* be altered in that way. But Trilling does not even entertain such an escape as a possibility in *The Liberal Imagination*. It is something he would consider, however, in later years. If the literature itself could be revealed as the dangerous beast, and if the murderous impulses latent within it could not be domesticated, was it worth protecting? In later years, when he looked more closely at the phenomenon of modernism, Trilling would have his doubts.

In the 1940's, however, the tasks he set himself were to enhance modern literature at its best and to reveal much emptiness elsewhere. Thus the Kinsey Report is criticized, in the wittiest essay Trilling was ever to write (p. 235), on the grounds that though "it brings light" (by virtue of the great number of facts it masses together, ". . . it is necessary to say of it that it spreads confusion" (by virtue of the fact that it does not understand the deeply human and complexly intimate nature of sexual intercourse). In another essay, Sherwood Anderson is gently rebuked on the grounds that he, unlike D. H. Lawrence, had no sensory and no social understanding of people. His world is vapid and given over to unqualified abstractions: ". . . the more he looks for their essence the more his characters vanish into the vast limbo of meaningless life, the less they are human beings" (p. 28). V. L. Parrington is insufficient because, though possessing many facts and a certain hold on "reality," he is devoid of ideas and hostile to thought. Parrington incorrectly believes, Trilling says, that ". . . there exists an opposition between reality and mind and that one must enlist oneself in the party of reality" (p. 8). Anderson, it is suggested, enlisted otherwise. Of American writers, only three, Fitzgerald, Henry James, and the Mark Twain of *Huckleberry Finn,* are open to the density of human contrariety out of which alone good writing can come. At his very best, Fitzgerald could pass his own test and "hold two opposed ideas in the mind, at the same time, and still retain the ability to function." Much self-deceived, of course, and profligate with his skills, he nevertheless understood, at least in *The Great Gatsby,* our wonders and our failures as Americans, and he could write with truth about both: ". . . the voice of his prose is of the essence of his success. We hear in it at once the tenderness toward human desire that modifies a true firmness of moral judgment" (p. 245). James, customarily considered ignorant of political reality, nevertheless gives us in *The Princess Casamassima* a portrait of political involvement that is astonishing in its perceptions. James understands, as proponents of facile progressivism do not, the costs of revolution: ". . . sometimes society offers an opposition of motives in which the antagonists are in such a balance of authority and appeal that a man who so wholly perceives them as to embody them in his very being cannot choose between them and is therefore destroyed. This is known as tragedy" (p. 77). And *Huckleberry Finn* is great, says Trilling (in perhaps one of the least ambitious and least moving essays collected in the book), because it holds in an unbroken vision the eternal beauty of the river and the perpetual squalor of shore life.

The American novel is otherwise a stunted thing. Only out of a study of manners and out of the penetrations of snobbery can the great novel arise. But if no manners, no novel. Echoing James on Hawthorne, he declares in "Manners, Morals, and the Novel" (1947) that there is in America "... no sufficiency of means for the display of a variety of manners, no opportunity for the novelist to do his job of searching out reality, not enough complication of appearance to make the job interesting" (p. 206). He makes more explicit what he has in mind when he says sharply in "Art and Fortune" that "in this country the real basis of the novel has never existed—that is, the tension between a middle class and an aristocracy which brings manners into observable relief as the living representation of ideals and the living comment on ideas" (p. 252). The thrust of this is to place life beyond ideals and ideas, to put it one step beyond any politics that would shrink it into pattern.

Almost all literary critics want, as I said earlier, the same thing; they want a literature that will "read" politics, not vice versa. The interesting twist that Trilling adds to this usual state of affairs is to argue that since life and art outpace politics by virtue of their complication, they must, at all costs, be *kept* complicated. If life and art disintegrate into easy order, the distance at which they stand from politics will be closed. Trilling's logic suggests, moreover, that politics becomes dangerous once it attains complexity. It then begins to resemble the very things whose superiority to it is supposed to be evident. Hence Trilling finds himself arguing, in "The Sense of the Past," for instance, that "the refinement of our historical sense chiefly means that we keep it properly complicated" and that literary scholars have an obligation to give to their studies "an appropriate complication" (p. 183). The quiet desperation of this line of argument is unmistakable. It bears, moreover, an unhappy similarity to Trilling's droll comment elsewhere in the same essay about those literary scholars who believe that "... for the study of history of ideas a really dead writer is better than one whose works are still enjoyed." Of such scholars, he says that "... we naturally pull up short and wonder if we are not in danger of becoming like the Edinburgh body snatchers who *saw to it* that there were enough cadavers for study in the medical school" (p. 177). In *The Liberal Imagination*, Trilling *sees to it* that literature is accorded the complications it must retain if it is to keep its primacy. Simplistic literature is, he says, just as distressing as simplistic politics. Ironically enough, those very politics, whether found in the 1930's or in the years of the Cold War and its inert factional quarrels, thus condition Trilling's literary sensibility. In *The Liberal Imagination*, he seems prepared to do anything to resist the shadow of politics, past and present. He beckons will to assist him. Yet politics, impelling him everywhere to make dense the complexities of literature and of life, nonetheless makes its claim upon him. By his resistance to politics, politics pulls him inward toward itself. Politics possesses, moreover, a latent power he is helpless to thwart. Should politics at any time deepen in its complexities, should it become any less the mindless dumb show of conflicting clichés it was in the 1930's and seemed to Trilling to be in the Cold War, then it would become, for him, dangerous in the extreme. His literary criticism supposes a political reality that is contemptible, not one that is inchoate and threatening. In the late 1950's and 1960's, then, when politics threatened to spill over the boundaries it was assumed to have in the pages of *The Liberal Imagination*, Trilling would encounter one of the hardest challenges of his career. He would be asked to determine the extent to which literature can yield complexities sufficient to encounter the new complexities of surrounding political life. He would be asked if a critical attitude formed in reaction to the doctrinaire simplicities of the 1930's could be wholly responsive to the powerful oddities of a later age.

8. The Supervision of Culture

The Liberal Imagination is, as we have seen, mindful of the danger posed by a politics that might become complex and, accordingly, not easily repudiated because it will seem to be like the very thing—literature—whose value is centrally based on its complexity and density. Hence politics is "best" when simply reprehensible, not when urgently demanding responses that only the subtle mind can give. However much Trilling interested himself in the reality of political life, he wanted that life kept in its place. If it were, the conflicts between literary sensibility and social sensibility could always be resolved in favor of the former. Hence, though his hostility to the New Criticism was abiding, and though he believed that that criticism was an attempt to anesthetize historical and political reality, he was not prepared to let a policy of utter laissez-faire govern that reality. That literature is a "criticism of life" is not to be understood as having a reciprocal truth.

The stability that Trilling wanted seemed momentarily possible in the early 1950's. The Depression and the crude pressures of the 1930's were gone, and the Cold War, although an intellectually bankrupt affair, was not the worst of circumstances. America, in short, had come to seem promising. It would, in fact, seem so to many until the very late 1950's. For these were "boom" years and a time of general economic prosperity. America even seemed attractive. England and Europe, tempting in earlier times, were not now clearly more attractive than the native grounds. The rough beast of history had apparently been tamed: "The American situation has changed. . . . There is an unmistakable improvement in the American cultural situation of today over that of, say, thirty years ago. . . . [We] are notably better off."[1] Thus Trilling in his contribution to the most important of the symposia that *Partisan Review* was to sponsor in the 1950's and 1960's, "Our Country and Our Culture" (1952–53).*

The reason he gives for his affectionate optimism about the United States, and for his readiness to be critical of attitudes simply assuming "alienation" to be part and parcel of the contemporary American intellectual's condition, is that the class of intellectuals had been joined by the class of money. Society was not now sharply divided into a party of money and a party of mind, a division that had in previous times generated problems of antipathy and resentment. The party of money had been the party of vulgarity and had implicitly supported the idea that concrete reality was the only true substance of American life. Theodore Dreiser had once been its voice in the world of letters. The party of mind, on the other hand, had repudiated material reality and had attempted to secure its foundations in abstractions alone. Its

---

*Trilling's enthusiasm for American possibilities did not mean that he was blind to the dangers of politicians who were opportunistically defending the "American way of life" at the time. In response to a 1953 McCarthyite investigation proposed for educational institutions like Columbia University, he led a number of his colleagues in saying that such an investigation would be unnecessary and harmful. It would be unnecessary because the number of teachers even once temporarily committed to Communism was negligible; and it would be harmful because it would create ". . . an atmosphere of apprehension and distrust that [would] jeopardize the cause of free inquiry and [threaten] the right to dissent, which is the foundation of civil liberties in a free society." Though Trilling and his colleagues felt that membership in Communist organizations did imply ". . . submission to an intellectual control which is entirely at variance with the principles of academic competence, as we understand them," they went on to argue that tests of such competence were an academic, not a governmental, concern. The "professional competence and personal integrity" of a teacher were, they said, the only matters of genuine concern. See *The New York Times*, Nov. 18 and 26, 1953. The other Columbia professors involved in drafting this position were Polykarp Kusch, professor of physics, Harold E. Lowe, director of university admissions, and David B. Truman, professor of government.

voice had early been heard in the works of Ralph Waldo
Emerson and later in those of Sherwood Anderson and in the
pleas of addlepated progressives. Only certain very powerful
artistic minds had been able to find a balance between such
extremes. One instance had been Henry James; F. Scott Fitzgerald had at least understood the problem, and had tried, in
his best fiction, to deal with it.

In the *Partisan Review* symposium, Trilling is prepared to
believe that the gap can be closed. Money and the education
it can buy had already done their work: ". . . the needs of our
society have brought close to the top of the social hierarchy a
large class of people of considerable force and complexity of
mind."[2] Looking with favor at the support given to Adlai
Stevenson in his campaign for the presidency in 1952,* Trilling praises ". . . the entry into our political and social life of
an ever-growing class which we must call intellectual, although it is not necessarily a class of 'intellectuals.' "[3] Money
and the desire for money were no longer, he suggests, providing the crucial distinctions in society.

He says, in effect, that the problems faced by American
culture were not now political problems. Political developments had somehow wonderfully meshed with the continuing
life of the mind: "Intellect has associated itself with power,
perhaps as never before in history, and is now conceded to be
in itself a kind of power."[4] The party of mind and the party
of money, growing together, could generate a cultural life
without the ugliness of political hostilities. The problems remaining, however, would be real and serious. They would be
the old problems, the kind Matthew Arnold had once con-

*Trilling, along with numerous Columbia colleagues, publicly endorsed
Stevenson's candidacy in a full-page *New York Times* advertisement on Oct.
16, 1952 (p. 21). This was seen, and meant, as a repudiation of the non-
intellectual candidate, Dwight Eisenhower, who had served as president of
Columbia University from May 1948 until the fall of 1950. Eisenhower and
the Columbia faculty had never arrived at comfortable terms of understanding.

sidered. Intellectuals must again be made to understand the complexity of the culture they inhabit. "It is possible," Trilling says, "that plans can be made for their welfare without diminishing their function. They can be trained. They can, I believe, be taught to think, or at least to think better." [5] To maintain, then, what he called "organic pluralism," lessons were to be imparted to intellectuals who, far from living at odds with their culture, now faced the opportunity and the challenge of living deeply within it. With doctrines of estrangement now obsolete, the situation was seen by Trilling as wholly anomalous: the self was held within the culture, the culture wholly surrounded the self.

This phase in Trilling's intellectual development is crucial. Remarkable for its optimism, it marks the point at which, as he saw it, the malaise affecting modern culture at its deepest roots, and not political conflicts within that culture, was to be thrust upon the intellectual consciousness. Intellectuals were showing that they were prepared to live equanimously within their culture. That he could see, and that he could value. But his optimism hides an enormously serious question, one that Trilling had again and again to turn over in his mind. What if culture, even in its fullness, could not sustain the life appropriate to mind in its highest capacities? What if culture itself were the zone of affliction? In 1945, thinking of Freud, Trilling had said *"We are all ill."* [6] What if the illness were now not so much of people themselves, people willing to enter fully into their culture, but of the situation that history had given them? Trilling's new-found optimism was made to meet new grounds for anxiety. Once again the dialectical seesaw of his mind was set in motion.

The literary studies he wrote in the early and mid 1950's, represented in the collections titled *The Opposing Self* (1955) and *A Gathering of Fugitives* (1956), are predominantly of the various ways in which the singular intelligence accommodates itself to the surrounding culture.* The argument implicit in both collections is that such adjustment was easier in earlier times. *The Opposing Self* deals "almost entirely with the nineteenth century," as William Arrowsmith said in a 1955 review, but is "written in solicitude for the twentieth."[7] Just as Arnold was once employed to set in perspective the superficialities of the 1930's, as England was once made to stand in contrast to America, as Forster once answered to the excesses of the will, and as conservative instincts were always made ready to chastise liberal ones, so here the past administers correction to the present. Trilling's strategy, here and elsewhere, is to lament the available, and to find attractions in the seemingly unattainable.

His 1951 essay on Keats (in *The Opposing Self*)—as fine, strong, and delicate an essay as he was ever to write—is at once a tribute to the poet's magnitude of humanity and a censure of the smallness to which the present age has been brought. The comparison could not be made more stark. Keats's "attachment to reality was stronger and more complex than ours" (p. 40); ". . . the life of art and intellect was then more genial than it is now" (p. 8); since his time "we have lost the *mystique* of the self" (p. 45). For a critic so disinclined to easy paradigms by which the self may be studied, and so hostile to systems that explain in a phrase or two, the Trilling who writes on Keats allows himself some large liberties. They are comparable to those taken, for instance, by T. S. Eliot. The "dissociation of sensibility" that Eliot brought to the attention of the literary world in 1921 was meant to show a decline in poetic power since Donne. The memorable phrasing is "A thought to Donne was an experience; it modified his sensibility. When a poet's mind is perfectly equipped for its work, it is constantly amalgamating disparate experience. . . . in the mind of the poet these experiences are always form-

---

*Page references to these two works in text will be preceded by *OS* or *GF* to avoid confusion; the editions used are *The Opposing Self* (New York, 1955), and *A Gathering of Fugitives* (Boston, 1956).

ing new wholes."[8] Trilling also sees a sharp break, but he dates it later. Keats, he says, " . . . did not . . . suppose that mind was an entity different in kind from and hostile to the sensations and emotions. Rather, mind came into being when the sensations and emotions were checked by external resistance or by conflict with each other, when, to use the language of Freud, the pleasure principle is confronted by the reality principle. Now, in Keats the reality principle was very strong" (OS, p. 31).

Trilling praises the "heroism" of Keats, his strength and health, his generosity of being and passionate regard for the elemental forces in existence. Keats possessed a fullness of character whose extinction marks the end of a phase in modern existence. For with the advent of modernity, a Keats is simply not possible. "He stands as the last image of health at the very moment when the sickness of Europe began to be apparent . . ." (OS, p. 49). At the center of Keats's heroism is his resistance to evil and its attractions. Such a stance, now impossible, defines the differences between past and present. Modern culture has allowed evil to penetrate, and then to saturate, the sense of self. We all yield to it. Keats, by contrast, was capable of offering evil his fullest recognition—he confronted horror and lived close to agony—without being overwhelmed by it. "Keats did not share in our acquiescence," says Trilling, ". . . to him the self was just as real as the evil that destroys it" (OS, p. 40). The equilibrium in which he gloried, an equilibrium he shared with Shakespeare, has given way beneath the insistent pressures that contemporary writers have set loose. Kafka, for instance, possesses true genius, but ". . . for Kafka the sense of evil is not contradicted by the sense of personal identity" (OS, p. 38). What is defective in Kafka is what is defective generally. Modern culture has led us to believe that what is most desperate and most perverse is most real. Speaking of the way in which "the imagination of disaster" displaces and devalues all other forms of imagination, Trilling moves to the heart of the argument he made again and again in the 1950's: "Our taste for the literature which arises from this imagination is a natural one, yet it has in it this danger, that we may come to assume that evil is equivalent to reality and may even come, in some distant and unconscious way, to honor it as such" (*OS*, p. 71).

Writing on Wordsworth in 1950, Trilling defines the new, and perverse, relationship into which modern culture and its imperiled audience have descended. He speaks of "our hyper-aesthesia, our preference for the apocalyptic subject and the charismatic style . . . " (*OS*, p. 148). It is a long way indeed from the magnificent sturdiness once possessed by Keats. He, bringing into play "negative capability," could allow himself to descend seemingly forever into peril and yet be out of danger. He *willed* not to know, and to be, everything. He ". . . remained with half-knowledge, with the double knowledge of the self and of the world's evil" (*OS*, p. 45).

Concluding the essay on Keats, Trilling brings himself around to the question any reader might have. What set this decline into motion? Trilling's response is both vague and inspirited. In fact, he refuses to answer that question and instead simply urges us onward. The maneuver and the effect could not be more Arnoldian:

We do not have what produces this tone, the implicit and explicit commitment to the self even in the moment of its extinction. Events, it would seem, have destroyed this commitment—and there are those who will rise to say that it was exactly the romantic commitment to the self that has produced the dire events of our day, that the responsibility for our present troubles, and for the denial of the self which our troubles entail, is to be laid to the great romantic creators. And even those who know better than this will yet find it all too easy to explain why Keats's heroic vision of the tragic life and the tragic salvation will not serve us now. . . . The spiritual and moral health of which he seems the image we cannot now attain by wishing for it. But we cannot attain it without wishing for it, and clearly imagining it. (*OS*, pp. 48–49.)

What does this mean? Apparently it means that Keats was

more right than we today can ever know. His heroic vision, involving at once a knowledge ot both the tragic and the healthy, is something we have to gain for ourselves. But Trilling knows we will not do so. He knows we cannot recover Keats's "Negative Capability," and that we will go on irritably reaching after fact and reason. We are impelled to do so by the excesses of our will. Modern culture draws us on relentlessly into its perversities. Of what possible solace, then, we might ask Trilling, are wish and imagination? Will not the sense of the unattainable only aggravate our plight? Does not the example of Keats serve only as a source of cultural frustration for us? Trilling seems to agree, but he nevertheless reaffirms the right and truth of struggle. Thus the doctrine of what he calls "the opposing self." That self is the one he praises.

As he defines it in the essays that make up his two books of the time, it is the self we might possess were we at the center of our culture, intimate with it and rank with its myriad details, and yet seeking forever to be freed of it. The opposing self thrusts itself away somehow from the culture that would imprison it, but is saturated with the vital qualities of that culture. In accommodating itself to what it sees as its handicap—its rootedness in the culture—it finds its heroism. Keats, with his idea of "soul-making, of souls creating themselves in their confrontation of circumstance" (*OS*, p. 45), exemplifies such heroism. Much of *The Opposing Self* and *A Gathering of Fugitives* is actually a search for other figures who may be considered heroic in the same sense. Against them, in an age Trilling sees as "ideological," we may measure ourselves.

When we see the figures he chooses, we understand that Trilling's sense of heroism is modest. He avoids the glorious. The examples of William Dean Howells, John O'Hara,*

---

*Writing an introduction to the Modern Library *Selected Short Stories of John O'Hara*, (New York, 1956), Trilling commented with great admiration on O'Hara's "passionate commitment to verisimilitude" and his "preoccupation with the social distinctions among people" (pp. viii and ix).

George Orwell, the "biological" Wordsworth, and the pains-
taking Flaubert of *Bouvard et Pécuchet* come to his mind.
The lackluster have, in his opinion, their own triumphs.
Speaking of Edith Wharton, for instance, and *Ethan Frome*,
which he does admit is a "dead" book, Trilling in a 1955
essay introduces us to his notion of the "morality of inertia."
That morality is something not to be praised, he says, but to
be recognized. The recognition consists in this: ". . . that
moral inertia, the *not* making of moral decisions, constitutes
a large part of the moral life of humanity" (*GF*, p. 37). Calling the phenomenon one with which literature has never
been wholly happy, and pointing out how its dullness and
stolidity have therefore been prettied up with "a certain high
grace" by some writers, Trilling is nevertheless much attracted to it. Much great literature has omitted mention of
it, but in doing so has not been wise. "Morality," he says, "is
not only the high, torturing dilemmas of Ivan Karamazov
and Captain Vere. It is also the deeds performed without
thought, without choice . . ." (*GF*, p. 40). Wharton portrays
it, but perhaps without intention or comprehension. Wordsworth, who took on enormous importance in the 1950's for
Trilling, portrays it, however, with the full understanding
that he is bringing to his readers a new moral code. The
morality in Wordsworth's best poems is identical, Trilling
says, with that ". . . conceived by the great mass of people in
the world." In that sense, it utterly lacks any artificial and
exaggerated qualities. It is ". . . the morality imposed by
brute circumstance, by biology, by habit, by the unspoken
social demand which we have not the strength to refuse, or,
often, to imagine refusing. People are scarcely ever praised
for living according to this morality—we do not suppose it to
be a morality at all until we see it being broken" (*GF*, p. 39).

Believing, then, that the heroism of a Keats is inaccessible
to the modern temperament, Trilling explores in the middle
1950's other ways in which a sturdy, well-balanced "attachment to reality" could be forged. The times needed no apoc-

alyptic hyperesthesia, no charisma. Against the perversities so
common in modern literature could be opposed a steady vir
tue. It would be a virtue that would not call attention to itself. The intellectuals who found themselves in the United
States at the time should, with Trilling, be pleased that the
class of intellect and the class of money had converged. But
they would also be well advised to see that the *here* and the
now must be acknowledged. Not to do so would be for them
to remain oblivious to the true roots of tragedy. Praising
Wordsworth, Trilling observes that: ". . . every tragic literature owes its power to the high esteem in which it holds the
common routine, and the sentiment of being which arises
from it, the elemental *given* of biology" (*OS*, p. 148).

To understand this rather complex turn of thought in
Trilling's mind, let us now turn to Wordsworth. In *The Prelude, Book Two,* he had described how he had been given, in
his seventeenth year, a "never-failing principle of joy / And
purest passion." This principle, derived from his observations
of nature in all its fullness, would protect him always in the
years thereafter. Trilling draws his much-used phrase "sentiment of being" from that moment in Wordsworth's poem
(lines 396–405):

> Thus while the days flew by, and years passed on,
> From Nature and her overflowing soul,
> I had received so much, that all my thoughts
> Were steeped in feeling; I was only then
> Contented, when with bliss ineffable
> I felt the sentiment of Being spread
> O'er all that moves and all that seemeth still;
> O'er all that, lost beyond the reach of thought
> And human knowledge, to the human eye
> Invisible, yet liveth to the heart. . . .

With Wordsworth thus in his mind, with "the sentiment of
being" in mind, and with his exaltation of the common routine, the burden of much of Trilling's writing in the 1950's

was a re-emphasis on the essentially *conditioned* nature of existence. He would hallow, as had Wordsworth, what *is*. He would persuade his readers in the *Partisan Review* and the *Kenyon Review*, and the members of The Reader's Subscription, who received its little publication *The Griffin*—in other words, his fellow intellectuals—to respect it. The distortions of modern literature—ravages would not be too strong a term—had provoked him to declare his faith in the utterly commonplace, the stuff of everyday existence. Without such faith, we would be drawn always on to violence and extremity. We would, he says in "Wordsworth and the Rabbis" (1950), ". . . imagine, with nothing in between, the dull not-being of life, the intense not-being of death; but we [would] not imagine being—we [would] not imagine that it can be a joy" (*OS*, p. 146).

It would be easy to observe at this point how, in an age well-known for its political conformity and quietism, an age tranquilized by the American president of the time and by the satisfactions of widely shared consumer affluence, Lionel Trilling went about creating a sophisticated means by which he and his fellow intellectuals, all the readers of the little magazines, could surrender to the status quo. Some evidence does indeed lead in that direction. Trilling did attempt, in "Wordsworth and the Rabbis," to persuade his readers of the triumphant visions of writers who had created figures ". . . intended to suggest that life is justified in its elemental biological simplicity" (*OS*, p. 150). He had indeed remarked upon certain writers, modern writers, who seemed to be at one with Wordsworth: Lawrence and his "primitive people"; the "curious silent dignity" of some of Hemingway's characters; Faulkner's black people, those who "endured." And in a 1952 essay he had praised George Orwell's respect for "the old bourgeois virtues." Orwell had seen revolution, had seen poverty and had known exploitation. But he had seen so much that he had seen through a great deal. Easy answers could not satisfy him, and he had come to believe that the older virtues were hard enough to practice without casting about for new ones. Such virtues were admirable because, as Trilling honestly put it, ". . . they were stupid—that is, because they resisted the power of abstract ideas" (OS, p. 166). But in all of this Trilling in the 1950's does not offer a counsel of resignation. His plea is not to give up the will. Abjuring revolution, frenzy, and apocalypse, he nonetheless does not recommend lassitude. Rather, he says that in Wordsworth, Lawrence, Hemingway, Faulkner, and Orwell the will is not extinguished but given a new domain in which to function. It no longer seeks its satisfactions in simply vying with the givens of existence. It fully accepts those givens and, *mirabile dictu*, is thereby freed from the hold they have. Once released, it pays full attention to itself: "At least as early as Balzac [he wrote in "Wordsworth and the Rabbis"] our literature has shown the will seeking its own negation—or, rather, seeking its own affirmation by its rejection of the aims which the world sets before it and by turning its energies upon itself in self-realization" (OS, p. 150).

The will, according to Trilling, pulses life into itself. It pursues its own understanding of itself down to the very core. Thereby it actualizes itself, enhances itself, and grows stronger. Stendhal's Julien Sorel learned at last to turn away from the impermanent attractions of the world and to live, for a short while at least, in a new awareness of the power of his will separated from society. Whatever politics in the 1950's this line of thought might encourage, it would certainly not be that of resignation. The wise citizen, without being partisan, should be self-aware and attentive. The wise intellectual should share these powers. Later in his career, particularly in *Sincerity and Authenticity*, Trilling would investigate this idea more closely and, in his fashion, would improve upon its paradoxes and complexities. In *The Opposing Self* he points the way to his later discussion by a reference to Hegel. He says that it was Hegel ". . . who first spoke of the 'alienation' which the modern self contrives as a means for the fulfillment of its destiny, and of the pain which the self incurs because of this device of self-realization" (*OS*, p. xi).

It is unfortunate that *The Opposing Self* does not explore any more explicitly than this what Hegel had in mind, or what such "alienation" implies for the modern writer or for his readers. Much more could certainly have been said—and needed to be said—for us to understand what Trilling was thinking about when he wrote so exultantly about how the will was to grow stronger by its acceptance of the givens of existence. But as soon as Trilling picks up this line of thinking, he abandons discussion of it.

The result is that his position on many matters in the 1950's is by turns excited, optimistic, and at last somewhat obscure. He says that the self gains knowledge of its own being by first learning of the force continually suppressing it. Until it knows that it has an oppressor, it cannot know itself. Once it comes to that recognition, however, it is provided with some intuitive understanding of how the relationship of self and oppressor will turn out. Thus it acquires a notion of fate. It then, in turn, gains the awareness that the relationship of self to oppressor, to the surrounding culture, can be negotiated in any number of interesting and vital ways. Moral awareness develops out of an evaluation of those ways, and aesthetic sensitivity grows out of a consideration of that moral awareness:

For Hegel [Trilling says] art is the activity of man in which spirit expresses itself not only as utility, not only according to law, but as grace, as transcendence, as manner and style. He brought together the moral and the aesthetic judgment. He did this not in the old way of making morality the criterion of the aesthetic: on the contrary, he made the aesthetic the criterion of the moral. (*OS*, p. xii.)

This description of Hegel is convenient indeed for Trilling as an admirer of Arnold. Hegel and Arnold both seem to be saying that literature is a criticism of life. When Trilling states, then, that ". . . the modern imagination of autonomy and delight . . ." makes ". . . a new idea in the world" (*OS*, p. xiv), he has in mind his belief, nurtured over the years, that while we go about reading books, those same books "read" us. Neither purely object nor subject, a work of art moves dialectically in relation with the stuff of life out of which it has come. This relationship, central to all aesthetic existence, is most powerful and urgent when the work in question is most deeply planted in the soil of circumstantial reality and particularity. Hence those writers who pay the greatest respect to the details of life, while being always conscious of the will to transcend them, are those who deserve our greatest respect.*

All of this would be well, in *The Opposing Self* and *A Gathering of Fugitives*, were Trilling to allow himself to describe in any detail the workings of the transcendental imagination in its actions of opposition and self-definition. Regrettably he does not. He raises complicated theoretical issues, but leaves them suspended. And he gives himself over, almost entirely, to a careful elucidation of how the sort of imagination he then preferred roots itself in mundane detail, and why it is to be congratulated for doing so. Thus the 1951 essay on William Dean Howells in *The Opposing Self*, in which that novelist is recruited to the cause of antimodernism.

Howells is praised there for his utter reliability as an American writer immersed in American ways, for his provincialism, for his "reasoned neutrality," and for his "intentional lack of glory." He is deserving of our respect precisely because he is not, say, Kafka. Kafka illustrates the ruination of those very "stupid," old-fashioned, and stable domestic virtues whose balanced deployment had given to Howells his drab

---

*An attitude toward art much more refined than the one expressed in 1940, when Trilling was uneasily attempting to maintain that art might exist beyond the here and now. He spoke then of ". . . the possibility which art offers of an experience that is justified in itself, of nearly unconditioned living." See "Literature and Power," *Kenyon Review*, 2, no. 4 (Autumn 1940), p. 442.

goodness. If, as Trilling says, "for Howells the center of reality was the family life of the middle class" (*OS*, p. 88), then modern writing may be defined as a concern with the same reality, but in a corrupted form. Modern writers have forgotten that bourgeois virtues are never to be exhausted, no matter how weak they have become. "Even today," Trilling says, "when our sense of family has become much attenuated, the familial theme shows its power in our most notable literature, in Joyce, in Proust, in Faulkner, in Kafka" (*OS*, p. 89). Why should we not praise, then, the original Howells, with his equanimity before the compelling circumstances of everyday life? Why praise Kafka and his distorted responses? Howells *knew* the family; Kafka knows only the perverted outlines of its former strength. If Howells makes much, in one novel, of hunting for a house, we should not pretend the subject to be beneath us, for ". . . it is a fact of spirit that it must exist in a world which requires it to engage in so dispiriting an occupation as hunting for a house" (*OS*, p. 93). Of course, ill at ease with Howells, we want to think such a subject beneath us, for ". . . the prototypical act of the modern intellectual is his abstracting himself from the life of the family" (*OS*, p. 163) and everything it stands for. Trilling's devotion to the quotidian in this essay, and elsewhere in these two books of the 1950's, could not be more strong. To be so devoted was for him a sign of genuine intellectual strength in that decade.*

---

*Joseph Frank's brilliant criticism of Trilling in the late 1950's was provoked by this devotion to the quotidian. Frank saw Trilling as ". . . one of the least belligerent and most persuasive spokesmen of the conservative imagination," and he said that Trilling, in maintaining his long-standing antipathy to the will, at last stood ready in the 1950's ". . . to endow social passivity and quietism *as such* with the halo of aesthetic transcendence." Frank wanted to remind Trilling, however, that ". . . not every evil is ultimate, not every acceptance is heroic. . . ." To glorify acceptance in such a way was to make no distinction between self-realization and a blind and dumb submission to destiny. It was also to confuse *any* given condition of life, even the most casual bourgeois convention, with the most sacrosanct conditions of life itself. Frank's criticism is well taken, but it was well taken by Trilling himself, and Frank gives short shrift to the tough contradictoriness of Trilling's mind. In his essay on Edith Wharton in *A Gathering of Fugitives,* the fine point of which Frank does concede, Trilling clearly sees the

The devotion on his part explains, for instance, his admiration for the sociologist David Riesman and his studies of American life in the 1950's. Riesman, with his claim on the actual, was doing just what novelists like Howells were traditionally expected to do. He was exploring the real terrain of society and reporting on its shape and feel. If writers infected by the modern sensibility cannot be expected to be responsible, at least the livelier sociologists like Riesman can. "Mr. Riesman," Trilling writes, "has the intrusive curiosity that is the mark of the classic novelist. The novelist, in his ideal character, is the artist who is consumed by the desire to know how things really are, who has entered into an elaborate romance with actuality" (*GF*, p. 93). Denis Donoghue complained in a 1955 review that Trilling was remarkably unliterary in his judgments and appreciations, was far more engaged by ideas than by literature, and was happiest "when roaming about the large triangle whose sides are Sociology, Politics, and Literature (in that order)."[9] This censure, issuing from an exceedingly narrow definition of the proper province of literary criticism, is nevertheless just when one considers the Trilling of the 1950's. With his Arnoldian fears and hopes, with his sense that modernity was a danger and yet that the decade was promising because of its stability and affluence, he seems to have believed that he, as a literary and moral critic of politics, had found a *supervisory* role in his culture. A delicate balance between the aspirations of domestic politics and the modern sensibility must be maintained. One demand must be matched against another. Indeed, it was the duty of the enlightened intellectual to guide these

---

danger of his restrictions on the will. "The morality of inertia, of the dull, unthinking round of duties, may, and often does, yield the immorality of inertia. . . ," he says; he then goes on to say "No: the morality of inertia is not to be praised, but it must be recognized" (p. 40). Trilling here seems to have anticipated Frank's criticism, and to have rebutted it. See Joseph Frank, "Lionel Trilling and the Conservative Imagination," in *The Widening Gyre: Crisis and Mastery in Modern Literature* (New Brunswick, N.J., 1963), pp. 268, 259, 260.

forces into proper alignment.* With these notions of "responsibility" and "superintendence" in mind, Trilling thus joined the ranks of certain other thinkers of the time. His ideas consorted well not only with Riesman's reconsideration of individualism, but also with other theories about the way in which the "mainstream of American life" should flow: with the views of "consensus" historians like his colleague Richard Hofstadter, "end of ideology" political scientists like Seymour Martin Lipset and Daniel Bell, and those social psychologists who had explained McCarthyism as an inflammation of "status resentment" and feared all turbulence in public and political life. Trilling, as a powerfully influential literary critic, as a friend and colleague of some of these thinkers, and as someone who was attempting to negotiate a passage more directly into the center of American life, argued that one must give oneself to one's society and grant it its particularities. Orwell had done so; John O'Hara had done so; Edmund Wilson had also once done so; why could others not now do so? As a member of society, a literary critic must certainly defer to the modern artist who estranges himself from his society in order to find himself. But the meritorious artist will find his way back to his society and to himself, and the proper society will at last embrace him—or so, as Trilling suggests in his neo-Arnoldian conception of society, things should work. Thus, with the 1950's in mind, he can say that "the pragmatic acceptance of society is morally possible, as Mr. Riesman of course knows, only under certain conditions. It needs an economic situation of at least relative prosperity,

---

*R. P. Blackmur made much the same point in 1950 when, in commenting on the impersonality of Trilling's style, he said it was the style of "the public mind," or "the mind of society." Blackmur saw Trilling as investing himself with the authority ". . . to take a position, to react and to respond, between incommensurable forces. He is an administrator of the affairs of the mind." See "The Politics of Human Power," in *The Lion and the Honeycomb: Essays in Solicitude and Critique* (New York, 1955), pp. 32–34. The essay was published originally in *Kenyon Review*, 12 (Autumn 1950), pp. 663–73.

and it needs a society which actually is tending toward democracy, a society with a high degree of mobility making for an increased equality" (*GF*, p. 97).

And, with the modern artist (namely Gustave Flaubert) in mind, he can say that: ". . . in each of the *Three Tales* [Flaubert] asks what remains when culture is rejected and transcended. The answer, given with a notable firmness and simplicity, is that something of highest value does remain—it is the self affirmed in self-denial: life is nothing unless sacrificial" (*OS*, p. 205).

Once again, just as in *The Liberal Imagination*, we see that politics must not be permitted to get out of hand, no matter how important it is. Affluence can assure stability, which in turn can inhibit the messy anarchies and internecine struggles that might, in their complexity, rival literature in its complexity. Unlike *The Liberal Imagination*, however, Trilling's writings in this later period suggest that the modern artist is to be regarded askance if *he* gets out of hand. A Kafka sorts ill with a Howells, and the twistings inflicted by the former on the homely virtues celebrated by the latter are a sure danger. Quoting Gide, Trilling reminds us (in 1949 in an essay on F. R. Leavis) of the peril he has always had in mind, namely ". . . a profusion of extreme passions which, by a sort of inflation, brings about a devaluation of all moderate sentiments" (*OS*, p. 103). Both politician and artist may be held culpable for such devaluation.

The critic, according to Trilling, must bring attention to danger and find a passage around it. Situated between the twin forces of political reality and cultural reality, he must carefully measure out proportions and adjustments between them as he sees fit. His duty is to balance things. The possibility of balance, moreover, now exists. And that is the basis for the peculiar hopefulness of Lionel Trilling in the 1950's. It is a muted, even a troubled, hopefulness. He knows as well as anyone that a historical moment may appear stable and yet be unstable. There is no doubt that he harbors deep anxieties about the situation through which, as a guiding intellectual, he is to provide a middle way. Those anxieties will grow in the 1960's. His book of that decade, *Beyond Culture*, will make those anxieties plain and mark the last major phase of his career.

9. The Adversary Culture and Its Discontents

LIONEL TRILLING'S ATTITUDES in the mid-1950's were those of a literary critic who had sought a condition of cultural stability, at times believed it could come into existence, but was nonetheless anxiously attentive to the forces that could hurl stability to the winds. Individual self and surrounding culture could achieve equilibrium—or so he then willed to believe for the first and last time in his career. The confidence occasionally flashing through the pages of *The Opposing Self* and *A Gathering of Fugitives* is, however, dimmed here and there. Trilling is conscious of the sinister encroachments of Kafka's modernity on Keats's premodernity. What successes will the man of the middle, the adjudicator, the supervisor of culture—Trilling himself—have if the situation lurches out of his control? What if culture cannot sustain the life of the mind? He knew that the situation would be "dynamic" —the "opposing self," that is, would seek constantly to draw away from a culture that it had already taken the trouble to comprehend—but he hoped the energies involved would not be destructive. That opposing self would explore its alienation and would, in Hegelian fashion, painfully achieve its destiny. The autonomous, transcendent imagination would flourish but would maintain its own security amid the commonplace. All would be well.

That it was not, that churning beneath the surface of American cultural life were turbulences that Trilling's model of supervision could not control, tells us something about the literary 1950's. They were not, as the decade itself was not, "tranquilized." Rather, the conformities, stupefactions, and silences of the time concealed forces utterly alien to any notions of stability. McCarthyism, the political movement by which the time is frequently defined, was led by a strangely refractory demagogue thoroughly unresponsive to any code of conformity or submissive compromise. He was, in fact, a dissident. And much of popular American culture of the time—Marlon Brando's and James Dean's dislocated heroes in touch only with highly personal codes of behavior, or the psychologizing of Robert Lindner's avidly read *Rebel Without a Cause*—attempted to engage indirectly the restlessness and violence beneath the apparent equilibrium of public surfaces.

By the time Trilling came to write the essays collected in *Beyond Culture*—that is, between 1955 and 1965—the unstable components of culture examined in the two earlier books had become more visible to him. Trilling is now besieged by doubts. He believes that the literature of modernity under examination in *Beyond Culture* has introduced, purveyed, and then *established* a sense of disaffiliation and resentment in the fabric of culture. Jane Austen long ago had sensed, he says in 1957, what large changes in society would mean to individual well-being: In "Emma and the Legend of Jane Austen" Trilling notes that she ". . . perceived the nature of the deep psychological change which accompanied the establishment of democratic society—she was aware of the increase of the psychological burden of the individual . . ." (p. 1).* Trilling, however, can no longer describe the situation simply as one in which the active heroism of a Keats has given way to the tortured passivity of a Kafka. Individual artists are not now so important as the structures of understanding built up around them. Thus Trilling's "adversary culture." Thus also his timorousness in its presence. That cul-

*All page references to *Beyond Culture* are to the Viking Press (Viking Compass) edition (New York, 1968).

ture he thinks of as a class, not in strict economic terms, but
in terms more important to him than those derived from
traditional class analysis. (Those terms, we know by now,
were never much countenanced by him anyway.) "Ours is the
first cultural epoch," he writes in "On the Teaching of Modern Literature" (1961), "in which many men aspire to high
achievement in the arts and, in their frustration, form a dispossessed class which cuts across the conventional class lines,
making a proletariat of the spirit" (p. 25). Thus, though this
"class" is adversarial and subversive in its intentions, and
though it derogates rationality and promotes "primal, non-
ethical energies" (p. 19), it is also well organized and ideol-
ogized. The "disenchantment of our culture with culture
itself" (p. 3) has all the look about it of an institution. It lives
on itself, promotes itself, and establishes its own pieties and
shibboleths. Elsewhere in *Beyond Culture,* in the 1965 essay
"The Two Environments," Trilling quotes, approvingly,
Saul Bellow's diagnosis of the problem: "Literature has for
several generations been its own source, its own province, has
lived upon its own traditions, and accepted a romantic separation or estrangement from the common world" (p. 230).

This situation would be, for all its paradoxes, still acceptable to Trilling were it not for certain distressing implications arising from it that act to question the primacy, and
moral efficacy, of literature. As he sees it, the modern situation will be a bad one if literature is granted its proper centrality in the culture *and* if that literature is perverse; on the
other hand, the situation will be just as bad if literature, no
matter how perverse its nature, is not given centrality. In
considering these equally bleak alternatives, *Beyond Culture*
therefore comes at last to have deep doubts about literature,
about art, and about their received uses. Something is deeply,
radically wrong about the present conjunction of all these
phenomena. Trilling believes that the adversary culture has
set down certain guidelines by which "autonomy of perception" may be realized; we are aware of the crucial importance

of such autonomy to him. It is what art had always promised,
a way in which the individual could be freed from the tyranny of culture while yet departing from that culture on knowl-
edgeable terms.* The problem with contemporary adversarial culture, however, is that it has learned to protect itself, and,
in self-protection, to conceal its working assumptions, some
of which are quite likely ulterior and sinister. Emile Durk-
heim and Max Weber had once celebrated the existence of a
"freischwebende Intelligenz," a free-floating intellectual class.
Trilling, in his own turn in the late 1950's and early 1960's,
was ready to celebrate the formation of such a class, but not
its unaccountability. Left to itself, that class might grow very
strong; and left to itself with only literature as its sustenance,
and taste-making as its power, it might become threatening
both to the culture surrounding it and to the art on which it
had prospered.

These anxieties sustain the pages of *Beyond Culture.* They
are not unlike the anxieties expressed then and somewhat
later by other thinkers of Trilling's generation, of his background, of (roughly speaking) his own class. By the end of the
decade of the 1960's—a decade in which faith in a "consen-
sual" model of society had been eroded by war, racial tension,
and generational revolt—many such intellectuals were ready
to express doubts, even hostile suspicions, about the culture
and the elaborate institutional apparatus in which they felt
it, and themselves, entangled. They were, like Trilling, uneasy about the ways in which art had been absorbed and es-

---

*And such autonomy was apparently possessed by the one group in the
country to which Trilling felt his deepest connection. The so-called "New
York intellectuals" had been a part of the larger cultural life surrounding
them, yet had achieved a fruitful separation from that life. "The class of
New York intellectuals is not remarkable for what it originates . . . ," Trilling says in the "Preface" to *Beyond Culture,* but ". . . as a group it is busy
and vivacious about ideas and, even more, about attitudes. Its assiduity constitutes an authority" (pp. x–xi). That, to Trilling, might constitute the best
of things: marginality combined with authority. As we shall see presently,
Irving Howe's notion of a tough-minded dissenting intelligentsia permanently policing the borders of society is like Trilling's notion of a detached authority.

tablished in society. To compare Trilling's doubts and wor-
ries, then, with those of, say, Daniel Bell, Irving Howe, and
Edwards Shils, as I shall presently do, is to understand his
anxieties more clearly. It is also to understand how he attempted ingeniously to negotiate a passage through a situation of acute cultural malaise.

Trilling takes the core of the achievement of the adversary
culture to be its attack on what he calls "specious good." That
attack, prolonged and brilliant, makes the literature in which
it is embodied profoundly spiritual. That literature seeks to
discover the truth of moral intimacies, to probe the roots of
unhappiness, and to inquire "if we are saved or damned" (p.
8). It comes at us through indisputably great literary works—
through those of Dostoevsky, Gogol, Proust—and it asks us to
declare ourselves with regard to the intensity of our lives.*
"Nearly overcome as we are by the specious good, insulted as
we are by being forced to acquire it, we claim the right of the
Underground Man to address the 'gentlemen' with our assertion, 'I have more life in me than you have' " (p. 81). This
kind of spirituality, about which Trilling is most wary,
pushes us bit by bit away from the doctrine of simple pleasure
that had nourished writers and readers in "pre-modern"
times. As he says in "The Fate of Pleasure" (1963), both
Wordsworth and Keats, for instance, could praise pleasure
and do so without ambivalence. For Wordsworth ". . . pleasure is abstract and austere, for Keats it is explicit and volup-
tuous" (p. 64), writes Trilling, but for both it is central and
desirable. The adversary culture has, however, now taught us
a new lesson. It has taught us the means by which we can
painlessly accommodate ourselves to the most horrific kind of
literature, while at the same time it has taught us to be sus-

---

*Interestingly enough to any reader sensitive to the ways in which Tril-
ling's argument often alludes but does not specify, there is no real grappling
with Dostoevsky, or Gogol, or Proust in *Beyond Culture*. Such writers are
mentioned, but whatever they happen to amount to, in their literary complexity, is not treated. Does Proust, for instance, actually ask us if we are
"saved or damned"? If so, how and where? Trilling never says.

picious about pleasure: ". . . our present sense of life does not
accommodate the idea of pleasure as something which constitutes the 'naked and native dignity of man' " (p. 58). Pleasure is too *easy*; pleasure, we have come to believe, blinds us
to a real understanding of *la condition humaine*. Hence we
tell ourselves that we must open ourselves to serious discomfort in our personal lives and, as Trilling points out in the
most heartfelt essay in the collection, "On the Teaching of
Modern Literature," in our classrooms, if we are teachers.
We are asked, and we ask ourselves, as living people and perhaps as living and teaching people, to expose and to scrutinize
what is most intimate to our selves, and openly to judge the
moral authenticity of those selves. As a pessimist about the
substance of human nature and its secrets, Trilling knows the
process will turn out to be tortured. In one of the most moving and passionate essays in *Beyond Culture*, that on Isaac
Babel (1955), he speaks of the secrets the heart and mind can
carry, and of their costs. Babel, a Jew and the son of a man
who had been a weak, disappointing failure, had had to confront the secrets of violence, of Cossack glory, and of physical
outrage. He did so, and he grew fascinated ". . . by what the
violence goes along with, the boldness, the passionateness, the
simplicity and directness—and the grace" (p. 137). He had to
give in to what Trilling calls his "feral passion for perception" (p. 140). Trilling knows that that passion is one to
which many modern writers—Lawrence and Yeats and even
Forster—have in our time surrendered. Our own imagina-
tions have been given intensity and nervous strength, but not
comforting pleasure, by those brilliant authorial surrenders.
We read, uneasily, the works that have issued from them. We
can end, he argues, by being seduced by them.

During the decade in which *Beyond Culture* was written,
social affluence was, as Trilling points out, still on the rise
and providing a greater degree of prosperity and immediate
personal satisfaction for American consumers. The phenomenon of "modernism" in the 1960's was, then, built on para-

dox. The teachings of society were encouragements to greater, more direct acquisitions of pleasure. But the high culture of the time was, in its institutionalized forms, in what Dostoevsky, Kafka, Proust, Babel, Lawrence and others had come to mean to Trilling, pointing to the hollowness of pleasure. Affluent people were prompted to see that pleasure was specious. Trilling puts it this way: ". . . another morality, which we may describe as being associated with art, regards with a stern and even minatory gaze all that is implied by affluence, and it takes a dim or at best a very complicated view of the principle of pleasure" (p. 67).

This distressing paradox is akin to the problem addressed by Daniel Bell in his book *The Cultural Contradictions of Capitalism*. Bell, who had once taught at Columbia with Trilling, agrees with his former colleague in many respects (quoting him on several occasions): "genius" has become democratized, accommodated, and institutionalized, no matter the intensity of the attack on traditional society mounted by such genius; and ". . . the search for release has become legitimated in a liberal culture and exploited . . . by commercial entrepreneurs . . ." (Bell, p. 145).* Bell says, moreover, that the avant-garde has triumphed in art and that he can no longer see any tension between new art that shocks and a society that is to be shocked. He thus places himself in sympathy with the Trilling unnerved by his Columbia students' ability to stare fearlessly into the abyss of modernity, to describe it easily, and to participate in what Trilling ornately calls ". . . the socialization of the anti-social, or the acculturation of the anti-cultural, or the legitimization of the subversive" (p. 26). Both Bell and Trilling see artistic modernism as a seducer, a force so powerful and authoritative in its blurring of older moral distinctions that almost nothing can stand in its way. And both are convinced that such modernism has

*Daniel Bell, *The Cultural Contradictions of Capitalism* (New York, 1976). Page references in text to this work will be preceded by the word "Bell" to distinguish them from references to *Beyond Culture*.

found its greatest strength during a historic moment when economic affluence is spreading and enhancing the lives of more and more Americans. To say the least, both are alarmed conservative critics of everything represented by modernism. One important difference does exist between them, however. Bell, in an argument rather coarse in comparison to that of his former Columbia colleague, places the "blame" for such a crisis on a collapse of the structure of beliefs justifying American capitalism. A doctrine of "the untrammeled self" (Bell, p. 144) has taken over; immediate pleasure-seeking has replaced older modes of delayed gratification. In a passage central to his book, Bell writes that contemporary American culture has been dominated ". . . by a principle of modernism that has been subversive of bourgeois life, and the middle-class life-styles by a hedonism that has undercut the Protestant ethic which provided the moral foundation for the society" (Bell, p. 84). His argument also includes a description of what he sees as *the* contradiction of contemporary society. Western industrialism has at last come into direct conflict with Western cultural expressiveness: " The one emphasizes functional rationality, technocratic decision making, and meritocratic rewards; the other apocalyptic moods and anti-rational modes of behavior. It is this disjunction which is the historic cultural crisis of all Western bourgeois society" (Bell, p. 84). One difference between the two writers resides, then, in their respective understandings of the fate of pleasure. For Bell, pleasure is the "old" pleasure, a pleasure of understandable, traditional gratifications. It is what everyone has always wanted but has been taught to deny himself under the pressure of forces such as the Protestant work ethic. Now it has been sprung loose, and social chaos is the consequence. For the subtler Trilling, on the other hand, pleasure has undergone a transformation. The "old" pleasure is now associated with "the specious good," and the spuriousness of such good has been taken for granted in the higher reaches of artistic achievement. There, the "primal, non-ethical energies" (p.

19) have been discovered and canonized. Nietzsche, for instance, teaches us that "the primal stuff" of great art is its "sadic and masochistic frenzy" (p. 19). We now seek not beauty and pleasure as they once were known, but their opposites; "we dread Eden" (p. 79). Our sensibilities live ill at ease with the sumptuousness of the physical surroundings that American economic progress has provided for us.

Irving Howe is more bitter in his denunciations of the cults of modern pleasure than is Bell, and more elegiac than either Bell or Trilling in his devotion to an older world unravaged by pleasure in either its aggrandizements or perversities. In his remarkably moving *Commentary* essay of 1968, "The New York Intellectuals: A Chronicle and A Critique," which is a somber summing-up of the achievements of the group of essayists, teachers, journalists, and artists in which he himself is now preeminent (and which Trilling once helped to make eminent), Howe sees that older world invaded by the youthful shocktroops of the mindless gospel of "unobstructed need" (Howe, p. 233).* Caring nothing for the past, which is hindrance itself, and in particular caring ". . . nothing for the haunted memories of old Jews," that newer generation wants instead ". . . works of literature—though literature may be the wrong word—that will be as absolute as the sun, as unarguable as orgasm, and as delicious as a lollipop" (Howe, p. 255). Such a generation is implicitly at war with Howe's generation, and Trilling's before it. The values of those earlier generations had been formed in the 1930's. Dialectical toughness, rationalism, enlarged political consciousness, and sharp moral conscience were at the center of those values. They have been given over, says Howe, to a farrago of authoritarian, elitist, anarchistic, and revolutionary doctrines randomly bound together by delusions of innocence and injections of

*Irving Howe, "The New York Intellectuals: A Chronicle and A Critique," reprinted as "The New York Intellectuals" in Irving Howe, *The Decline of the New* (New York, 1970). Page references in text will be to the book version of this essay, and to other essays in the same book, and will be preceded by the word "Howe" to distinguish them from references to *Beyond Culture.*

amnesia. His language in describing that "new" generation could not be more bitterly polemical, and his feisty pessimism owes nothing to Trilling's style of discourse, but the substance of his argument shares certain elements with that of the author of *Beyond Culture*.

Both Trilling and Howe remark on the disadvantage at which they have apparently been placed by the onslaught of "the young." Trilling fears being seen as an "eccentric . . . obscurantist and reactionary" (p. 6) by the students to whom he is to teach modern literature. Those students who, under his tutelage, stare comfortably into the abyss, might soon come to see their teacher as no more than "old, respectable, and bald" (p. 11). Trilling feels himself to be of that same ". . . generation facing assault and ridicule from ambitious younger men" that Howe describes, a generation "in process of being lost . . ." (p. 214). For Howe, the attack means that whereas his generation had become scattered and proudly individualistic despite its common origins, it is now unified in its distress: ". . . the rekindled sense of group solidarity is brought to a half-hour's flame by the hardness of dying" (Howe, p. 214).

Howe sees, as does Trilling, that the New York writers, though they might once have constituted an intelligentsia in the classic sense—perhaps the *only* intelligentsia in the United States conforming to Russian criteria of advanced critical thought, active opposition to the status quo, and a sense of apartness—have now degenerated into an "Establishment" that finds its greatest enemy to be its own success. By virtue of its own ambitions, its subsequent achievements, and its whetted taste for triumph, it is now comfortably assimilated into the social reality it once aspired to repudiate. Just as the ethnic group from which many of its members had come—immigrant Jewry—has now been absorbed into mainstream American life, so *it* has been absorbed. Howe's elegiac spirit, in this celebrated essay and in some others of the time, thus unites both a solemn reverence for a neglected tradition and a sociological observation Marcusian in its irony: "Bracing enmity has given way to wet embraces, the middle class has discovered that the fiercest attacks upon its values can be transposed into pleasing entertainments . . ." (Howe, p. 16). The result everywhere to be seen is "overwhelming cultural sleaziness" (Howe, p. 264).

The disgust is Howe's; it is not Trilling's. For if the irony of the situation is apparent to both, they appraise that irony differently. To Howe, the conclusion to be drawn is that modernism has at last defeated itself and a great, if marginal, tradition has vanished. For modernism is not itself if it is not marginal; in "The Idea of the Modern," an essay of 1967, Howe sets down as law, in his own italics, the notion that *"modernism must always struggle but never quite triumph, and then, after a time, must struggle in order not to triumph"* (p. 6). The best of intellectual life is to be spent, as he would have it, in *dissent*. Trilling is not so sure. A curious tone now and again entering the pages of *Beyond Culture* comes from his suspicion that the paradoxes of the situation have not yet been exhausted. The drama has not ended. Where Howe bleakly sees the end of modernity, the "Decline of the New," the Trilling schooled by Hegel sees the possibility of new syntheses growing out of old oppositions.* In

*One indication of Trilling's openness to new possibilities, both cultural and political, in the mid-1960's is revealed in his attitude then toward Stalinism and Communism. He wrote in 1958, in a passage typical of his thinking then, of ". . . the emptiness and inhumanity of Stalinist Marxism" and said that ". . . Stalinist Marxism, under whatever name, is essential to Russia." (See his "Introduction" to *The Broken Mirror: A Collection of Writings from Contemporary Poland* [New York, 1958], p. 10.) In 1967, however, he found himself objecting to Communism not on moral but on political grounds. Calling himself an anti-Communist, he nevertheless said that he could understand why an underdeveloped country could plausibly turn to Communism and discover strength there. There are, he said, ". . . occasions when the political tradition of a people [makes] democracy impracticable" and this fact ". . . has to be accepted." Trilling's acceptance is based on hopeful meliorism; he can imagine ". . . that the authoritarian aspects of such governments as I here envisage will come short of totalitarianism. . . ." See his contribution to the symposium "Liberal Anti-Communism Revisited," *Commentary*, 44, no. 3 (Sept. 1967), p. 76. It is this capacity for movement, change, and moderate

the "Preface" to *Beyond Culture*, he puts the idea with a capaciousness of insight and a stubborn optimism that are foreign to Howe, at least the Howe of 1968:

. . . how else are civilizations ever formed save by reconciliations that were once unimaginable, save by syntheses that can be read as paradoxes? It is often true that the success of a social or cultural enterprise compromises the virtues that claimed our loyalty in its heroic, hopeless beginning, but there is a kind of vulgarity in the easy assumption that this is so always and necessarily (p. xv).

The search for some such new synthesis underlies the bulk of the essays collected in *Beyond Culture*. Trilling attempts to secure a position wholly responsive to the sociological and cultural realities he observes but not submissive to them. Again, he wants to read *his* culture; he does not wish simply to be read by it. The posture to gain is the posture of equanimity.* It is an attempt in which he will allow many of his suspicions about literature to accumulate, in which he will turn, as we shall presently see, to powers of the mind not aesthetic in nature. He will turn, that is, to a power he calls "truth." It will be praised as something superior to mere beauty and aesthetic pleasure.

Before examining the ways in which that "truth" is pursued, the views of the celebrated Chicago sociologist Edward Shils are worth examining. Shils is in essential agreement that the 1960's saw a shattering of forms, an enlargement of sensibility, a dissolution of social restraint, a drive toward some kind of peremptory personal authenticity, a decline of reason—in short, an onslaught of "antinomianism." As a

---

flexibility that distinguished Trilling from some of those intellectuals in whose company he is frequently located.

*This notion is illuminated when he says in "The Fate of Pleasure" essay: "Our typical experience of a work which will eventually have authority with us is to begin our relation to it at a conscious disadvantage, and to wrestle with it until it consents to bless us. We express our high esteem for such a work by supposing that it judges us. And when it no longer does seem to judge us, or when it no longer baffles and resists us, when we begin to feel that we *possess* it, we discover that its power is diminished" (p. 71).

professional student of intellectual classes and their formation, Shils could write in 1964: "One of the more remarkable
developments of recent years in the West is the assimilation
of the culture of the avant-garde in the more routine and
even philistine cultural circles" (Shils, p. 130).* Thus he is in
basic agreement with Howe and Bell, and with Trilling,
about the present fate of the adversary culture.

The tougher tone he contributes to an understanding of
the situation, however, involves the belief that intellectuals
have traditionally been an irrelevant or irresponsible entity
(as he puts it in the essay "Intellectuals and the Center of Society in the United States," ". . . the intellectuals in the last
two-thirds of the nineteenth century had practically no positive influence in American society" [Shils, p. 194]), and that
intellectuals may be defined by the spirit of alienation they
nurture, so that their absorption into society is extremely
dangerous. They threaten the "real" elites of the society and,
by virtue of their new proximity to the centers of power,
present a demonstrable hazard to the proper functioning of
American life. After all, intellectuals will not, or cannot,
wholly give up what Shils calls their "penumbral traditions,"
by which he means their hostility toward established authority. Those traditions have ". . . retained their vitality despite
their several decades of submergence, and in the recent troubles of the political, administrative, and military elites, the
tradition of alienation has been reactivated" (Shils, p. 194).

Shils's recommendation in the face of such danger is remarkable, and frightening, in its no-nonsense lucidity: the
real elites must maintain the upper hand and must consoli-
date true power in American society. If, as he says, "the legiti-
macy of the executive elites . . . has been impaired" (Shils, p.
194) by a more antinomian and expressive culture, then that

*Edward Shils, "The High Culture of the Age," reprinted in Edward
Shils, *The Intellectuals and the Powers and Other Essays* (Chicago, 1972).
Page references in text will be to the book version of this and other essays,
and will be preceded by the word "Shils" to distinguish them from references
to *Beyond Culture*.

culture must be neutralized. Universities are the proper
agent of such neutralization, for they are, after all, the arena
wherein the conflict can now most vividly be witnessed. Moreover, universities contain disciplines truly faithful to the best
interests of American society as a whole. Those disciplines are
"objective." By that Shils means that such disciplines function in accord with "the political, administrative, and military elites." He concludes his argument on the matter by
saying: "The stability of the larger society depends, therefore,
on the maintenance, within the culture and the institutional
system of the intellectuals, of the predominance of that element which accepts an objective discipline and the integra-
tion of academic institutions into the central institutional
system of American society" (Shils, p. 195).

Shils is significant here because, on a matter crucial to
Trilling—the disposition of an adversial aspect of culture—
he takes an extremely hard line. His views may be compared
to those of others we have considered. Bell sees the situation
as dynamic and worrisome, but his is a fairly neutral account
of how the three realms of modern Western society are ad-
justing to one another, ruled as they are ". . . by contrary
axial principles: for the economy, efficiency; for the polity,
equality; and for the culture, self-realization (or self-gratifi-
cation)" (Bell, p. xii). Howe bitterly laments the passing of a
rigorous, but marginal, intellectual style now the victim of
cheap adulteration and easy accommodation. Neither Bell
nor Howe proposes a response to the situation; the social
scientist, aware of the pluralisms of his society, establishes the
categories by which they may be identified; the elegist per-
fects what, after reading Howe's celebrated essay, Robert
Lowell called his "tact and tough, ascetic resonance."[1] But
Shils does have a proposal: keep the hostile intellectuals, and
their adversary culture, in check. Accommodate them—but
only after they have been neutralized.

For all their obvious differences in tone, in language, and
in sensibility, Trilling and Shils are united in one important

way: they want a resolution of the problem they observe. Howe and Bell appear satisfied, at least in the key writings studied here, in describing the exhaustions and contradictions. In now returning to Trilling and *Beyond Culture*, we see that his attempt at a resolution is, as we might by now expect, elaborate and intricate. Its substance is to be found at the heart of *Beyond Culture*, in the 1963 essay "The Fate of Pleasure." In it he reminds his readers that the literature of modernity with which he is concerned is a *moral* literature whose strenuousness and painful honesty are virtues we may associate ourselves with proudly. That literature may be at war with the specious good, but we can admire "the energy, the consciousness, and the wit" it possesses. Unlike Shils, therefore, Trilling cannot bring himself to hope for a neutralization of that literature and the general irresponsibility it might provoke within the larger social enterprise. Such literature might, in fact, be the only thing left to us as thinkers about which we can feel admiration. "Upon it," he says, "we base whatever self-esteem we can lay claim to—it gives us . . . our 'last distinction'. . . . Can an adversary scrutiny of it point away from it to anything else than an idiot literature . . . ?" (pp. 79–80). Of course we have now learned not to respect any such idiot literature, with its "positive" heroes and shallow affirmations. We have learned to travel with Dostoevsky's Underground Man and, even at the cost of appearing only fashionable, to ally ourselves with "that extruded, 'high' segment of our general culture." It has an "exigent, violently subversive spirituality" and with it we are protected from the surrounding culture that "we hate and fear" (p. 80). In explanation of the title of his collection of essays, Trilling says that we have thus been granted the means to stand "beyond culture."

Saying that, however, Trilling goes on to reveal how uncertain he is about the entire matter. On the one hand, he believes that we must be prepared to pay those high costs of socializing ourselves that Freud, in *Civilization and Its Dis-*

contents and elsewhere, argued were inevitable. He also believes, along with Arnold, that we must acknowledge our responsibilities to society. And yet he concedes that Freud's price might be too high, and that ". . . the loss of instinctual gratification, emotional freedom, or love" might very well *not* be ". . . compensated for either by the security of civilized life or by the stern pleasures of the masculine moral character" (p. 24). What, then, are we to do? Stand ready to be welcomed, with all of our bizarre and suspicious-looking intellectual baggage, into that valley of idiot literature lying below the "extruded 'high' segment" of culture? Or attempt to secure a station "beyond culture," making sure that in doing so we do not become merely faddish? He means, I think, that we should certainly go "beyond culture." But what, precisely, does he mean by "beyond"?

He means at least three different things by the term. His meanings do not, however, easily sit side by side with one another. For that reason *Beyond Culture*, as we shall see, is at its very center a confused book. To begin with, Trilling suggests that "beyond" be given a political meaning. Perhaps the distressing situation intellectuals now face would be resolved if they would consider modernity to have a political substance. They could then clothe that substance in an appropriate politics of the world. He makes such a suggestion while candidly recognizing that for typically modern literary people, and particularly for those living in the American 1950's, political life is likely only to evoke "disgust and rage." In writing later, for instance, about the celebrated Leavis-Snow controversy, he accuses Snow of being ". . . at one with the temper of intellectuals today—we all want politics not to exist, we all want that statement of Hegel's to be absolutely and immediately true, we dream of reason taking over the whole management of the world, and soon" (p. 164). But Trilling knows better than this. In "The Fate of Pleasure" essay, he knows, and confesses he knows, that modernity expresses a demand that is rational and positive and that ". . . may have to be taken into eventual account by a rational and positive politics" (p. 84). Politics *does* exist; it *must* be in the accounting.

But in making such a proposal, Trilling unwittingly returns himself to the same dead end he had entered years before in writing *The Liberal Imagination*. Seeing in that book that liberalism was thin and inadequate as a political philosophy, he could not turn to the prospects of conservatism, for they were even more sterile and implausible. It was only certain conservative sentiments, and not conservative doctrine, that he allowed himself to value. Two decades later, the problem is much the same. In pondering, then, ". . . those psychic energies which are linked with unpleasure and which are directed toward self-definition and self-affirmation," he rightly says that they ". . . demand a gratification of a sort which is not within the purview of ordinary democratic progressivism" (p. 85). He is then left to imagine a kind of politics that might gratify them. The problem, however, is that such antinomian energies are appropriate only to an antinomian politics, the very politics a Lionel Trilling would face with dread.

Caught in this dead end, Trilling turns to the later, meta-psychological writings of Freud for help. Perhaps, he thinks, some understanding can be found there about the nature of a politics suitable to modernity. The answer he receives is not a welcome one; by the same token it is not a surprising one in light of what we have already learned of Trilling. If society is faced with the troubling presence of psychic energies linked with unpleasure, those energies may be understood in terms that Freud would give them. Let us say, then, with Trilling, that we now ". . . confront a mutation in culture by which an old established proportion between the pleasure-seeking instincts and the ego instincts is being altered in favor of the latter" (p. 86). And if, with Trilling's help, we pursue the arguments of Freud's *Beyond the Pleasure Principle* (1920), we see that such an alteration is perverse and morbidly ill-founded for the very reason that ". . . the other name that Freud uses for the ego instincts is the death instincts" (p.

86).* Having thus followed Trilling's line of reasoning, we would be disposed to agree with him that when we speak of a politics appropriate to modernity, we must have in mind a politics of death.

This, then, is one meaning Trilling gives to "beyond." A hint of the meaning was given long before, we recall, in his story "The Other Margaret" and in his novel, *The Middle of the Journey*. There, considerations of death displaced all temporal and local considerations. In the long run, the story and the novel imply, John Maynard Keynes was indeed right, and we shall all be dead. And under death's shadow, the politics of social melioration are but a passing fancy. After all, in concurring with Freud that the aim of all life is death, Trilling also says that we must acknowledge that ". . . the organism wishes to die only in its own fashion." And, writing in 1963, he concludes his own meditations on pleasure's fate and on a suitable politics of modernity by adding a characteristic note to Freud's dicta. He says that Freud was right about death but that the organism wishes to die ". . . only through the complex fullness of its appropriate life" (p. 87).

Such considerations, all too morbid, and hence apparently all too unattractive to him, lead Trilling elsewhere in *Beyond Culture* to posit another definition for the phrase "beyond culture." If a political meaning leads nowhere but to a political cul-de-sac, perhaps a metaphysical meaning will prove

---

*Or so Trilling erroneously thought. A more careful, and accurate, reading of Freud would have shown him that the link between the ego instincts and the death instincts was never made direct and clear. *Beyond the Pleasure Principle* is, in fact, the moment when Freud abandons the ego instincts and adopts the more useful death instincts: "Our views have from the very first been dualistic, and to-day they are even more definitely dualistic than before —now that we describe the opposition as being, not between ego instincts and sexual instincts but between life instincts and death instincts." (Sigmund Freud, *Beyond the Pleasure Principle*, trans. James Strachey [New York, 1961], p. 47.) The death instincts and their conflict with the life instincts, in other words, supplanted in importance the conflict involving the ego instincts in Freud's metapsychology. And Eros and Thanatos were never wholly reconciled in that metapsychology with the earlier terms. For a discussion of this complex issue, see Richard Wollheim. *Sigmund Freud* (New York, 1971), pp. 203–13.

more rewarding. He proceeds to generate that meaning in the first essay in the book, "On the Teaching of Modern Literature," by noting that Keats and George Santayana were skeptical about art, about its power, and about its prestige in society. They had, that is, tried to go beyond culture in their own ways, and in an earlier time. Keats's skepticism is misunderstood or neglected, Trilling says, because it does not seem to tally with his modern reputation. But Keats, says Trilling, was nevertheless the poet who once wrote to his brother George that there was something more important than poetry, for it is ". . . not so fine a thing as philosophy— For the same reason that an eagle is not so fine a thing as a truth" (p. 29). Keats thus had his doubts, even if his modern adulators do not, about the value to be granted to the ephemeral contrivances of the "creative" mind. They are no substitute for *the truth*, for it can survive the local instances of its telling. Having permanence, it soars above the culturally defined, in this case classes, professions, and history. In a burst of euphoria, Trilling tells us that it was once like mind itself, belonging to nothing "but to man" (p. 176). He ends *Beyond Culture* by enthusiastically quoting twice again the same fragment from Keats's letter about truth and the eagle that he had used in the first essay in the book.

Trilling's intention here is once again to locate a station beyond the circumstantial hurly-burly into which art and its corrupting fashions have fallen. Maybe art has at last revealed its inadequacies. The concluding essay in *Beyond Culture*, "The Two Environments: Reflections on the Study of English" (1965), asks ". . . whether in our culture the study of literature is any longer a suitable means for developing and refining the intelligence" (p. 232). But this attempt on his part to go "beyond culture" and to leave literature behind is just as hazardous and dubious as was his earlier one to find a politics appropriate to the antinomian, adversarial, and deathly aspects of the culture he fears. Robert Mazzocco has pointed out (in a review of *Beyond Culture*) that John Keats showed more faces to the world than the one Trilling was ready to see, and that if Keats were to be quoted by Trilling in one way, he could just as easily be quoted by Mazzocco in another.[2] Keats might at times have been interested in the permanent *truth*; but at other times he was apparently just as interested in the impermanent fancies of his mind. He really cannot now be recruited to the cause of questioning the adequacy of literature. "The only thing that can ever affect me personally for more than one short passing day, is any doubt about my powers for poetry—I seldom have any, and I look with hope to the nighing time when I shall have none," wrote Keats in another letter to his brother (Oct. 14–31, 1818).

The fact of the matter is that it is not at all easy to apprehend a "truth" severed from its circumstances. Indeed, Trilling had been saying so for his entire career. He had tried for years to teach his readers that the complex particularities of a given life in a given time make up the substance of any worthwhile literary work. To those particularities every reader and, in fact, every citizen must pay attention if he is to understand the work. Literature is of substance and merit in a culture, but it is *in* that culture. Hence Trilling had for years chastised liberals for ascending to a vast empyrean of abstract ideas unanchored to particularities, for removing themselves from the life around them. Their affinity for pure "truths" was part of their shallowness and their innocence. Yet here, in the argument at the heart of *Beyond Culture*, Trilling seems to nourish within himself that same affinity.

His final effort in *Beyond Culture* to give meaning to his key phrase comes in his discussion of Freud's ambivalence toward the idea of culture. Though Freud may have taught us all that we are involved in complicated cultural processes— in family, tribe, and larger ritual everywhere—he also taught us, Trilling says, to beware the depth of our implication in culture. We participate constantly in the idea of culture yet, being human, withhold our complete assent to that idea. In his 1955 essay "Freud: Within and Beyond Culture," Trilling says that Freud had early recognized the roots of the present-day "adversary culture" when he saw ". . . the self as set against the culture, struggling against it, having been from the first reluctant to enter it" (p. 107). The present-day schisms in the cultural structure represent the final accumulated strength of that tension. For Freud, moreover, it is simply impossible, under any circumstances, for a human individual fully to enter culture. He cannot do so because he is primarily a biological and not a social entity. He is not infinitely malleable, not wholly responsive to the demands of his culture. The social being is a human being: "fastened to a dying animal / It knows not what it is." For many critics of Freud, this positing on his part of an irreducibly biological man is a demonstration of his conservative, even reactionary, posture. In Trilling's opinion, it is no such thing. It is a demonstration that Freud had found a way to lead us out of the imprisoning walls of society and culture. Freud's belief in biological foundations is, says Trilling, ". . . so far from being a reactionary idea that it is actually a liberating idea. It proposes to us that culture is not all-powerful. It suggests that there is a residue of human quality beyond the reach of cultural control . . ." (p. 113). Trilling's strategy here is not one that should surprise us. He had some years before argued that it would be possible to regain will by a surrender to circumstances. Now he argues that it is possible, paradoxically, to find freedom in a full acceptance of "biological fact."

What Trilling may now in retrospect be seen as doing is arguing, in *Beyond Culture*, against a school of neo-Freudian thought current after the Second World War. That school, identified with such figures as Harry Stack Sullivan, Erich Fromm, and Karen Horney, had de-emphasized biology and the "instinctual roots of man." It adhered to Marxist notions of social determination and social engineering. And it sought to argue for the "social" as the real area of human liberation. Not "biological fact," but "social fact," would be the answer. In the long and reverent essay on Freud in *Beyond Culture*, on the contrary, Trilling hovers admiringly and hopefully around "biological fact," imputing to it an ability to resolve the quandries into which our own culture has plunged us and a power to transport us beyond the confines of its ruins. Our identities of last resort will then become manifest. Our shackles of social definition will be broken. Trilling avails himself of a rhetoric almost Lawrencian in describing the process: "We reflect that somewhere in the child, somewhere in the adult, there is a hard, irreducible, stubborn core of biological urgency, and biological necessity, and biological reason, that culture cannot reach and that reserves the right, which sooner or later it will exercise, to judge the culture and resist and revise it" (p. 115).

All of this would be satisfactory, one supposes, if Trilling could supply us with any clear sense of the composition and powers of that irreducible core within each of us. He cannot do so. Nor can he persuasively argue that biological liberation will be any less hazardous than many of the other forms of liberation our culture spasmodically proposes to itself. "Biological fact" might have its urgencies and its necessities, but it surely does not, *pace* Trilling, have its "reason." Moreover, if we consider such a "fact" strictly in terms of its possible political manifestations, we can imagine just how unpredictable, how irresponsible, how ruinous it might turn out to be. "Historically or psychologically," Mazzocco writes, "man has always possessed such drives, and if they have not prevented tyranny in the past, why should it be assumed that they will do so in the future?"[3] Trilling's enthusiasm for such a means to go "beyond culture," an enthusiasm to which he apparently resorted only after other means to make the same journey had proved unreliable, seems a contrived and, at last, an indefensible enthusiasm. It is a gesture and apparently no more, a gesture "beyond." The kinds of rational, and not merely rhetorical, strengths that he should have employed if his anxieties about the adversary culture were to have issued in anything clear and positive are simply not in evidence in *Beyond*

Culture. In that book, he fastens with tenacity on tensions rooted far below the surfaces of contemporary cultural existence; he likes and does not like what he holds up to his inspection. The forces are "dark," the complications forbidding. He sets himself to solutions, but his impulses to resolve, by some transcendent mechanism, the entire burden of modernity take him one way, and then another, toward nothing in particular.

It is, in fact, "nothing in particular" that Trilling is later to entertain as a truly decisive means to put an end to the contradictions he so powerlessly observes in *Beyond Culture.* No great imagination is needed to see that his reverence for the immutable "biological fact" might in time have led him to yet another way by which he could hold death in reverence. The antithesis to biological fact is, of course, biological death. The conflict constantly waged between life and death is one that Trilling, attentive to Freud, had mused upon for years. If "biological fact," then, cannot actually release us from time and history, class and condition, passion and place, then perhaps life's counterpart can. The "sentiment of being" that finds its primordial identity in biology can just as well be defined, to Trilling's satisfaction in the Freud essay, in the cessation of biological life. That is why, in that essay, he can praise "the assertion of the death instinct" as ". . . the effort of finely tempered minds to affirm the self in an ultimate confrontation of reality" (p. 99). Literary art, he believes, can no longer liberate the individual from the tyranny of culture; once it had that power, but it has now been eroded. Nor, he says, can such art even be depended upon to tell the truth "or the best kind of truth" (p. xvii). With art reigning tyrannically, and with art not cleansed of its duplicities, the criticism of art has in time defaulted on its own special duties. Modernity is a kind of demon god, and Trilling says the occasions are few when it has been met "on its own fierce terms." Of modern literary criticism, as he and others have practiced it, he says that it has done little more than instruct us in ". . . an

intelligent passivity before the beneficent aggression of literature" (p. 231). We know only how to read certain books, not
how to *engage* them.

Perhaps truth, then, and genuine liberty are to be secured
not through art or through society or through criticism, but
through an avenue whose bleak vistas are defined by Freudian
ideas united with sentiments from E. M. Forster. Freud taught
him the truths of death. Forster taught him the virtues of
passivity. In *Beyond Culture*, Trilling learns to combine the
lessons.

Of Freud, Trilling writes that he needed to believe that:

> . . . there was some point at which it was possible to stand be-
> yond the reach of culture. Perhaps his formulation of the death-
> instinct is to be interpreted as the expression of this need. "Death
> destroys a man," says E. M. Forster, "but the idea of death saves
> him." Saves him from what? From the entire submission of him-
> self—of his self—to life in culture (p. 108).

Some three years after *Beyond Culture*, Trilling will expand
on such gracefully grim remarks. He will in 1968 bring his
thinking, refined by Freud and Forster, into conjunction with
his thinking on James Joyce.* We recall that the lessons of
Forster had expressed what Trilling believed in the early
1940's about the strange diseases of the fully empowered will.
Such a will could erupt, act provocatively, and disfigure
human and aesthetic situations. Forster had envisioned a
genuine moral life growing out of the ability of people to
"connect"; Trilling in turn saw that such connections could
not be forced but must issue from the slow fermentation of

---

*An earlier essay on Joyce, "The Person of the Artist," is a rather incon-
sequential attempt to come to terms with this centrally important modern
writer. Trilling does argue, however, that Freud and Joyce may usefully be
discussed together: ". . . the two men were in many respects very like each
other. They share the avowedly heroic intention and the ability to wait long
for achievement and fame. They share a fierce, isolate pride, and the need for
loyalty. They are at one in point of family feeling, especially in the disillusioned attachment to the father. And they share the paradox of being revolutionary in their work and rigorously conventional in their lives. . . ." (*Encounter*, IX [August 1957], p. 78.)

the peculiarly human. One *subsided* into truths of the moral life. In the presence of that life, Forster recognized little of worth beyond it. He gave his famous two cheers, and no more, to the secondary issues: governmental forms, national passions, the great public causes. About his central concern—personal morality—however, he was wholly positive. No traces of the century's familiar nihilism informed his thought on this matter. Nor does nihilism enter into Trilling's conception of Forster.

Both Forster and Joyce cause Trilling to examine the uses of the will, the value of the moral life, and the kinds of credence rightfully due the world. The responses Trilling makes to the two novelists could not, however, be more different. The movement from a concern with Forster to a concern with Joyce marks the progress, on Trilling's part, to a more direct confrontation with modernity. Joyce represents that modernity fully, and what he sees as the problematic nature of modernity is felt everywhere in his writing. Forster encourages Trilling, in 1943, to believe in the solidity of the world of moral good and moral evil inextricably joined. Joyce, in 1968, makes that world evaporate. This is not because Joyce introduces a persuasive immorality into Trilling's thought. It is because he introduces a form of nihilism that Trilling finds irresistible.

Trilling had for a long time seen that his moral criticism embraced an eschatology of sorts. What was his concern with death, in *Beyond Culture* and the books before it, if not a way of saying that, in the long run, certain strivings were finally quite unimportant? We "progress" in life toward certain death. So much, then, for progressivism. And what was death, in *Beyond Culture*, if not the ultimate resolution of all those taxing contradictions his criticism of modernity had illuminated? Forster had wanted to preserve the preciousness of those human intimacies encountered along the way toward final extinction. Thus his merit. Joyce, however, was skeptical about any such preciousness and any such interim value. His

eye, Trilling believed, was on the extinction of all value, final
and interim.

"Here I conclude," Trilling quotes Joyce as saying in a
late letter to his son, Giorgio, "My eyes are tired. For over
half a century they have gazed into nullity, where they have
found a lovely nothing."[4] Trilling takes such a declaration as
characteristic of Joyce, even though he allows that Joyce was
not much given to making large statements about ultimate
meaning. In contrast to Forster, Joyce as an artist had proceeded with the merely human within him burnt out; he had,
or so Trilling argues, "departed this life"[5] and found a way
to function purely in terms of his creative will. He had, Trilling claims, denied the world and its transitory claims upon
him; he had also denied the claims to real existence that the
world makes on its own behalf. In the "Ithaca" episode of
Ulysses, Joyce sums up the reality and the meaning of Leopold Bloom's existence by saying of him "That as a compe-
tent keyless citizen he had proceeded energetically from the
unknown to the known through the incertitude of the void."
Joyce believed in the *void*. He believed it was there and that
it yawned before all of us. As against Forster, Joyce was saying
"*Only disconnect*" and was, with an "indomitable egotism"[6]
that Trilling finds titanic and awful, exploring both the se-
ductive powers of entropy and the impulse to make nullity
prevail. Joyce had, in short, seen through life, seen through it
all. Trilling rightly calls such an achievement chilling, but
he cannot deny the peculiar majesty of its attractions for him.
Joyce, after all, was doing no more than representing, in a
novel, what readers of novels had come at last in this century
to believe: "That the world is a cheat, its social arrangements
a sham, its rewards a sell."[7] From what Trilling calls "our
moral infancy" we perceive this elementary truth. Where
readers of Dickens or Balzac might once have toyed with the
societal world, giving credence to it while at the same time
pleasurably withholding assent from it, we utterly reject that

world and the giant mirage of its value. Thus Trilling's conception of Joyce

It is a wholly unsettling portrait—not least for the reason
that the beautiful fastidiousness of Trilling's style, its large
and gracious modulations, is at the service of doctrine almost
empty of value. Trilling, an apostle of Arnold and Forster,
and attentive to the suppleness by which they both had allowed a world of moral gravity to ride comfortably on their
prose styles, is brought by his own doctrine of final things, in
which death is preeminent, to laud a writer who, he says, has
utterly plunged out of moral consideration. What, we ask,
can sustain Trilling's praise of Joyce?

The answer for Trilling seems to be the answer he supplies
for Joyce. Trilling is sustained in the late 1960's, as Joyce was
once sustained, by the capacity he has to measure the world
fully and carefully, never to divine its secrets too quickly,
never to come upon its truths prematurely. Joyce allows himself the fullest amplitude in entertaining the complexities of
the world; then he finds the world vacuous. Then and only
then. His genius rests on an exalted kind of patience. Trilling's craft as a critic does likewise. Mr. Leopold Bloom and
Stephen Dedalus are allowed to be as large and as curious as
imagination will let them be. André Gide had once written
"Please do not understand me too quickly." In his ability to
resist any foreshortening of imaginative possibility, Joyce ex-
tends to his characters the kind of solicitude Gide had asked
for himself. Along the way to emptiness, he can thus find
much with which to be preoccupied. Trilling, fascinated by
what he has found, puts it this way: "Joyce can be understood
to say that human existence is nullity right enough, yet if it
is looked into with such a vision as his, the nothing that can
be perceived really *is* lovely, though the maintenance of the
vision is fatiguing work."[8]

Fatigue, then, and the exacting pursuit of detail by which
the variousness of life may be measured and reconstituted,

and patience, and solicitude: such qualities define the Joyce
whom Trilling praises. Trilling grants Joyce the power to
effect a great reversal, or synthesis: "to move through the
fullest realization of the human, the all-too-human, to that
which transcends and denies the human."[9] We recall that
Trilling himself had years before made much of Hegel's belief that the modern self achieves its fulfillment by means of
the alienation it pursues. Joyce does not deny the process; he
simply reverses it. He pursues all the varied forms of fulfillment visible and manifest in the world but exits on the other
side of them. The art involved in such a pursuit consists in
not arriving by any shortcuts at nullity: "The fair courts of
life still beckoned invitation and seemed to await his entrance.
[Joyce] was to conclude that their walls and gates enclosed
nothing. His genius is defined by his having concluded this
rather than taking it for granted, as many of the generation
that came after him have found it possible to do."[10] With a
similar patience and solicitude, and with his own complex
fullness of comprehension, Lionel Trilling made his judgment in the troubled 1960's about what the walls and gates
of modern life contained. He saw, richly, that they contained
a nullity. He recognized, as did Joyce, "the nothing in particular" at the center of life around him.

It would be improper, however, to conclude here and to
allow Trilling's reading of Joyce to pass unchallenged. Joyce
usually has a way of entering the last word, and even one
after that, in consequential matters. It is true enough that he
had found that the gates and walls of life enclosed nothing,
and true enough that he had stared into nullity, there to find
"a lovely nothing." But there, with that recognition, Joyce
characteristically did not rest. If he was to move through one
great reversal, or synthesis, from the all-too-human to that
which transcends the human, he could just as easily go back
the other way. We recall that his last, great, book begins only
where it ends, and thus advances precisely nowhere; but it

does so not amid inspissate gloom but with a song, a woman's voice, the water of life forever running, a "funferall" in progress, and a notice that "Here Comes Everybody." It is fair to say that Trilling's Joyce does not shine forth with these comic plenitudes. Trilling heard only the doleful Joycean music.

10. *Sincerity and Authenticity*: Literature and Will

THE DIFFICULTIES, successes, and disappointments of Lionel Trilling's last major work, *Sincerity and Authenticity* (the 1969–70 Charles Eliot Norton Lectures at Harvard, published in 1972), sum up the difficulties, successes, and disappointments of his long career. The book is his most considerable achievement after *The Liberal Imagination* in 1950, and his most sustained work after *Matthew Arnold* in 1939. It comprises a history of the elaborate development of mind and self since Shakespeare, a brief consideration of certain literary texts he sees as central, a polemical refutation of some prophets of our time, and an authorial credo that conceals hope about literature while it counsels stoic resignation about life. And as his last argument with the forceful reality of death, it is also Trilling's attempt to discover a means by which the estrangement of self from self might at last be resolved.

The ambitiousness of such an undertaking is muted by the characteristically sinuous passivities of Trilling's style. No insurgent "I" moves through the pages of this book, but a "we" whose best side—informed curiosity, patience, wise understanding and invulnerability to surprise—constitutes the compliment Trilling seductively had paid to his readers for years. The desires of this writing self are assumed to be corporate. Its successes and its inadequacies are taken for granted as joint ventures. But part of the difficulty of *Sincerity and Authenticity* is that its strategy is both generous and insidious. It is the same in this book as it has been in his others: to argue by means of an abstract terminology whose meaning is presumed to be accessible to everyone but that is actually something the author alone controls and whose separate units he introduces and partially defines as the appropriate occasions arise.

In past writings, such terms have included, for example, "liberalism," "moral realism," "the opposing self," and "complexity." These are not vaporous terms, but their existence is dependent on a life that rhetorical employment gives them. They are customarily made to stand in opposition to other terms, equally conditional; together the active consort of all such terms provides the substance of the particular argument. To press strenuously for precise definition of a given term, to the exclusion of all other terms, is to press too far. Thus, as we have already seen, "liberalism" is not defined as a specific body of political doctrine when Trilling puts it to use in the 1940's and 1950's. It is only partly political, only partly moral, only partly social. It is, for rhetorical purposes, two things: a "good" liberalism and a "bad" liberalism. The former is inspired by Montaigne, the great hopes of the French Revolution, Mill, Arnold, and the nineteenth-century novel. This liberalism, "*ondoyant et divers*," is friendly to aspirant and revolutionary individualism. "Bad" liberalism issues from minds sunk into willfulness, progressive clichés, and imprisoning systems of political machination touted as benevolent, and from the suffocation of thought beneath the pressures of an obsessively militant concern with social circumstance or "conditions." The American middle class and its literary tastes sustain this lesser liberalism. What in sum, then, is "liberalism" to Trilling? It is what his strategies make of it.

The same problem may be traced through the pages of *Sincerity and Authenticity*. The key terms of that book are given a variety of interpretations, but this variety never shapes itself into a clear system. "Sincerity" is not seen steadily and whole; neither is "authenticity." Rather, the differences between them are to be noted whenever a given historical situation is evoked, and those differences are rooted in the active

and dialectical opposition of term against term: the one becomes itself through opposing the other.

This is, of course, the strategy of anyone who argues. Absolutely stable foundations are secured only when all the
primary terms are defined, but that stability is very difficult
to produce. When Trilling operates in his notably contingent
and dialectical manner, moreover, he is giving himself philosophical authority. Hegel is behind his arguments. As "self"
may be said to be defined by estrangement and opposition, so
terminology may be established through verbal opposition.
The irony of this procedure in *Sincerity and Authenticity* is
that even "authenticity" itself is subjected to contingency and
mutability. There is, as it turns out, more than one "authenticity" in this book; there are several. There is an *authentic*
authenticity (perhaps the Conrad of *Heart of Darkness* is its
exemplar); there are lesser authenticities (some forms of latter-
day psychotherapy are cited). The definitions each requires
are entangled in the book. *Sincerity and Authenticity* may
therefore be seen as a pursuit, on the part of both its author
and its reader, of the most compelling and genuine manifestations that fearsome reality can take. The reading is impeded,
however, by Trilling's wayward or backward glances toward
the lesser authenticities, and the different kinds of appeal each
exerts on him.

Trilling refers, late in the book, to Sartre's argument in
Being and Nothingness that psychoanalysis is a classic example of "bad faith." It treats the single self as composed of
". . . one part of the psychic whole regarding the other part
as an object and thereby disclaiming responsibility for it."
The consequence of such bad faith is that "exposing the inauthenticity of the mental life is itself ineluctably inauthentic" (p. 144).* Trilling seems open to the same kind of charge.
His style and his methods, fashioned and elaborated over the
course of a long career, and so responsive to ceaseless trans-

---

*All page references to *Sincerity and Authenticity* are to the 1972 Harvard
University Press edition.

formation, are strangely inappropriate to that impulse on his part to come at last to final terms with authenticity. His "bad faith" arises as he attempts to secure a fixed meaning for authenticity by employing a procedure that is relativistic. That procedure nonetheless governs the shape of Western cultural history as given in this book. Beginning its most complex and imposing phase of development some 400 years ago, that history, as Trilling sees it, is a movement in which the virtue of being sincere (like Shakespeare's Horatio, for instance) has deteriorated while the compulsion to be authentic (like Conrad's Kurtz) has grown like a virus. Trilling sees the moral life in process of revising itself and notes that such revision, in which a more strenuous and "exigent" moral life has supplanted an acceptant and genial one, has been nothing less than "a mutation in human nature" (p. 19). But mutations of this order, embracing as they do the individual, his society, his arts, his self-consciousness, and his relationship to authority of every sort, act to retard or prevent judgment of them. And that fact has Trilling worried. The relentless drive toward authenticity, as he describes it, clearly has as an ultimate purpose the destruction of any terms useful in defining authenticity. Trilling's critical endeavors in this book do not stand out of the way of such relentless destruction. He himself does not wholly control all the terms he sets in motion. Moreover, Trilling does not seem able to maintain a position in which he might unambiguously observe that destruction. He mixes favor and regret, acceptance and reservation, in the face of such absolutism. And how does he observe the rise of authenticity? With approval or with censure? Is authenticity now pure, or is it only one day to become pure? Can authenticity be seen clearly, or is it always to be obscured by the lesser authenticities, the spurious and counterfeit versions? Is the force of authenticity apocalyptic or dialectical? Will it emerge at last as something benevolent, or does it spell ruination? These and many other such large and speculative, but nonetheless appropriate, questions can be posed of *Sincerity and Authenticity*, but no clear answers to them are forthcoming. The book, for all its large scope, is more provocation than thesis. A long, troubled, and brilliant rumination, it yields few explicit conclusions.

Some readers might think this is so because *Sincerity and Authenticity* is a product of the 1960's, a decade of extraordinary division and tension, particularly in the very community of academic intellectuals that was Trilling's home all his life. It might be argued that Trilling was forced to see that the familiar and nourishing stabilities of American intellectual life, his time and his place, were to be no more.[1] The "adversary culture" had gained control; "reality" had conquered "mind"; once again the cruder aspects of liberalism were asserting themselves. Thus, the argument might run, the sustaining dynamism of Trilling's teaching at Columbia had been swallowed up by events at Columbia. The complexity of his long negotiations with many terms once found in an arena of mental struggle had been forced back into the confines of a simple political struggle, and he was left with nothing but rhetorical struggle and, at last, rhetorical emptiness.

This argument seriously misjudges both the strengths and the weaknesses of Trilling's customary way of dealing with local realities. Although he was physically close to events at Columbia in the late 1960's, and although he was aware of similar events at other campuses across the nation, he never seemed intellectually close to them. Interviewed at Columbia in 1968, he expressed the opinion that all of the issues at stake in the crisis at his university were, by turns, "factitious," "gratuitous," "adventitious," or "symbolic."[2] His attitudes were akin to those of William Butler Yeats when he said of the First World War that "We should not attribute a very high degree of reality to the Great War."[3] Trilling's ideas and his obscurities in the late 1960's do not seem a result of the events of that decade. After all, as every reviewer noted, and as by now we should be able to agree, he had been putting forth most of the ideas, and many of the key terms, in *Sincerity and*

Authenticity for his entire career. And his argumentative posture, in book after book, had always embraced more than it
could ever resolve. His last book is different only in the
strengthened desire it has to study closely the disturbances of
authenticity. In *Beyond Culture* he had already studied, we
recall, the distance between his own generation and those suc-
ceeding it. In the 1950's he had examined the ways in which
self could come to oppose self. Like many another critic,
Trilling had for years been establishing a vision of things
that would prove resilient to changes in local circumstances.

The transformations observed in *Sincerity and Authenticity* are therefore very large indeed. Trilling is insulated from
the small. The concern out of which everything else in this
book grows is taken from Freud, and late Freud, the Freud
of *Civilization and Its Discontents*. Trilling describes the
concern this way: ". . . society, though necessary for survival,
corrupts the life it fosters" (p. 60). Such an observation evokes
at once the historical, the social, the psychological, and the
tragic. It issues from an understanding that the knowledge of
greatest importance is self-knowledge, and that the self is now
imperiled by "external" forces. It implies that the self wants
to be at one with its own primary constituents, that it wants,
in a word, autonomy. It agrees with Hegel that the nature of
Spirit is to seek "existence on its own account," and to do so
at any cost. One of the costs is, in fact, its own interim estrangement from everything that might work to constrain it.
Perfect selfhood is unattainable but was once approximated
by the other virtue discussed prominently in this book: sincerity.

Yet sincerity, no matter the strength of its appeal, is seen
by Trilling as a lesser attribute. It is less awesome, less magisterial, less compelling. Now it serves us only as a reminder,
an artifact, of what autonomy once was in culture—but in a
culture to which we cannot return. Trilling's argument is
thereby historical in a basic sense. It understands what our
becoming cultural reactionaries would entail, and so admon-

ishes us not to take that step. We cannot go back to a culture of sincerity, and unless we wish to enjoy the absurd giddiness of the ahistorical life, we must go forward into authenticity. The gist of Hegel's declarations about the forwardness of Spirit prods us to do so, just as do the lessons of Freud that tell us that the superego will become ever more imperious, the mind ever more tyrannical of what it will extract from being, the conventionalities of human reason ever more tenuous, the nature of the human condition ever more "immitigable" (p. 156). Our most serious literature, be it Conrad or Dostoevsky, Isaac Babel or Céline, cruelly confirms that we are correct in what we have already intuited about our desperate state. Hence it is not a literature to be "liked," and Trilling certainly does not rest easy with much of it. But it decisively acts to drain color away from the literature to be liked, and it displaces the old literary pleasures and benefactions just as peremptorily as authenticity has displaced sincerity. It seems to have all the better arguments.

Another important sense in which Trilling's thinking in 1970 is historical lies in its hostility to the fashionable modern argument that only the here and now are real, and that the past has become irrelevant. Trilling cites the historian J. H. Plumb's argument that ". . . industrial society, unlike the commercial, craft and agrarian societies which it replaces, does not need the past. Its intellectual orientation is towards change rather than conservation, towards exploitation and consumption" (p. 137). With the death of the past, as so rumored, narrations of all sorts are gutted of their substance; the individual has difficulty in entering the self of any other by means of an enticing story; Freudian analysis fails because it depends on narration; Marxist analysis fails because it can no longer draw on the iron "logic of history"; and the family is weakened because it is no longer called upon to tell the child of his beginnings.

But Trilling will not succumb to this particular negative authenticity. He asserts his independence from it by maintaining a strong, even dogmatic, line of narrative intellectual history in this book. He describes what has happened to the self and the surrounding culture with extraordinary brevity and with a terminology that is stark in its binary workings. "Sincerity" and "authenticity" utterly fill his landscape. His style serves of course to add complexity and richness to that landscape. At times, however, it confers on it an unwarranted atmosphere of awesome difficulty. The main thrust of Trilling's narrative account is, after all, traditional and straightforward. He says that the moral, psychological, and social selves that we could once imagine ourselves possessing have been eclipsed. At some time in the past they were whole, and now are split into fragments. A "dissociation of sensibility" has taken over, and the concord that some moments in Shakespeare and other writers propose is now impossible. It was one "between me and my own self: were ever two beings better suited to each other? Who would not wish to be true to his own self?" (p. 4).

This wish evokes for Trilling a recurring vision of the perfectly autonomous self, wholly at ease with all its capabilities and enjoying a "sentiment of being" that, among writers, Wordsworth and Rousseau had once celebrated. (Wordsworth and Rousseau, always crucial to Trilling, become heroic in this book.)* But if the possibility of imagining

*As he attempts to portray them as heroic, he also attempts to draw them into close conjunction, particularly in their use of the all-important phrase "sentiment of being." Wordsworth certainly does employ the phrase, in *The Prelude, Book Two.* But in the sources used by Trilling, Rousseau unfortunately does not. The closest he comes, in the translation that Trilling cites, is to say ". . . the sociable man . . . knows how to live only in the opinion of others; and it is, so to speak, from their judgment alone that he draws the sentiment of his own existence." (Jean-Jacques Rousseau, *The First and Second Discourses*, ed. R. D. Masters, trans. R. D. and J. R. Masters [New York, 1964], p. 179.) Trilling silently changes the last word, "existence," to "being" when he quotes. The result is a closer parallel than the textual evidence permits. See also Laurence Lerner's review of *Sincerity and Authenticity* for his comment that, in the effort to join Rousseau to his arguments about "sentiment of being," Trilling misrepresents Rousseau and disorts his meaning. Lerner argues, moreover, that the associations Trilling advances between Rousseau and Jane Austen simply do not exist ("Past and Present," *New*

such an autonomy once infused literature and actual selves, and if even today we have a strong vestigial desire that the artist grant us a vision of the sentiment of being, we know that the costs of socialization have made such an enterprise impossible. That is the lesson of Diderot's *Rameau's Nephew*.

Trilling declares that book to sum up "the intellectual life of Europe for a century" (p. 27). The claim is extravagant, but *Rameau's Nephew* does ask us to consider the awesome force of society as it encroaches upon the individual. And the book inaugurates, at least for Trilling, a process to be traced throughout Western literary culture at its highest level: the movement of the individual beyond the strictures of morality and into a "freedom" allowing him an elaboration of his personality, an invigoration of his self-consciousness, and the chance to put on display the full potential of his being. But herein lies a paradox: this "freedom" cannot be resisted; it comes from the pressures of society, the very society thought to be transcended. Trilling thus sees the "freedom" of society growing to be a terrible force in Diderot's time. It assumes a complexity that places at a disadvantage the mere individual who attempts to exist in simple selfhood, and sincerity, within its midst. The disadvantaged self, like the poor nephew of Rameau, vaingloriously tries to respond to each and every demand society makes upon it. But it finds it cannot succeed, and so redoubles its effort by creating aspects of its own being—subselves or roles—to meet the confusing challenges it confronts. Rameau's nephew learns, as Trilling says, to become everything; he ". . . sounds all the instruments, enacts all the roles, portraying all the emotions in all voices and all modes" (pp. 32–33). He does go beyond moral categories, for he leaves behind him no moral center that might

---

Statesman, Oct. 20, 1972, p. 559). The lesson here is that complex historical and intellectual issues are usually blurred in books as brief as *Sincerity and Authenticity*. For further confirmation of the fact that Rousseau and Wordsworth see "sentiment of being" in very different ways, see the chapter by that title in Margery Sabin, *English Romanticism and the French Tradition* (Cambridge, Mass., 1976), pp. 103–24.

be thought responsible to such categories. The terms of his surrender to society are spelled out by his alienation. "It is social man," says Trilling, "who is alienated man" (p. 30).

Trilling's argument on this score bears a likeness to Richard Poirier's recent discussion of the modern "performing self." Poirier argues with exuberance on the topic (where Trilling argues with his customary darkness) and says:

By performance I mean, in part, any self-discovering, self-watching, finally self-pleasuring responses to the pressures and difficulties I've been describing. . . . When a writer is most strongly engaged by what he is doing, as if struggling for his identity within the materials at hand, he can show us, in the mere turning of a sentence this way or that, how to keep from being smothered by the inherited structuring of things, how to keep within and yet in command of the accumulations of culture that have become a part of what he is.[4]

Trilling would agree with this, but would go on to say that the casualty rate involved in such an ordeal is much higher than Poirier supposes. "The self-discovering" to which Poirier refers does not come easily, and Rameau's nephew does not bring himself to self-possession. The alienation that begins in surrender, is maintained as a means of self-preservation, and ends at last in an autonomy of self and circumstances perfectly combined, happens frequently to break down along the way. The wastage, the detritus, and the failures of much of modern culture are one kind of evidence of this fact. So also is the example Trilling chooses from literary history: Goethe's Young Werther. Werther endures alienation and the pain of culture, and he conforms to the teaching of Hegel's historical anthropology that sincerity is not deserving of his respect. He therefore rightly chooses disintegration. His only error, however, is in not letting it proceed far enough. He becomes a suicide, and Trilling's moral is that, as "a disintegrated consciousness, [Werther] had persisted in clinging to the simplicity of the honest soul" (p. 52). The moral is there for all of us to absorb. Werther had not understood that, at some absolutely crucial moments, there is simply no self to be true to. In those moments, sincerity becomes out of the question.* For Hegel and for Trilling, purest authenticity, authenticity pursued to its essence, provides the only way that the spirit may return to itself and become itself.

The major shift in history that is Trilling's subject in *Sincerity and Authenticity* is attributed (but only vaguely so) to actual historical causes. We are by now familiar, if not wholly content, with the kind of history Trilling writes. Its outlines are blurred, its movements bulky, its ambiance abstract, its directions always large and inevitable. Such a style is maintained in this book. If we are to be convinced by Trilling's history, it will be because of the persuasiveness of its general emphases and intuitions, its gestures and prophecies, and not because of its few hard facts. And this, we understand, is a serious liability in a book whose thesis is, after all, historical. We know that it is rhetoric, experience, and wisdom moving us, not the precise logic of historical argument.

One such emphasis and large movement, as treated by Trilling, is the growth of the idea of society. The feudal order dissolves, the Church loses its authority, cities come into being, and what Marx called "the idiocy of village life" is challenged. Urban populations grow dramatically and within their midst appear intellectuals. Trilling concentrates his attention, and no small part of his suspicion, upon them. They do not come into being in either kingdom or commonwealth, but only in the ". . . swarming of men in cities, in *Schwärmerei*, as Carlyle called it" (p. 20). Edmund Burke, whom Trilling does not mention, had noted the same thing, and his anxieties predated those of Carlyle. Intellectuals,

---

*Another example appropriate to Trilling's argument here would be the unknowable, and unknowing, self at the center of Julien Sorel's being. For a particularly acute examination of that lack of a self for Sorel to be true to, see Michael Wood, *Stendhal* (Ithaca, N.Y., 1971), p. 77: "Julien is above all an unknown quantity, and partly because the character he presents is in any case an artifact, a composition, a montage of borrowed bits and pieces."

thought Burke and his successors, have no function other than to examine society, "to scrutinize the polity" (p. 26). By conducting their examinations, they define society, for society is that body of individuals endowed with the greater self-consciousness given to it by its intellectuals. Trilling sees intellectuals and the ever-developing awareness of self they provide as the cause, the germ, of modernity. But since he does not see modernity as a blessing, he looks at intellectuals and all they have brought about with ambivalence. He had for long distrusted the "adversary culture," yet had recognized its inevitability. The same frosty recognition is extended here to intellectuals, and we are reminded of his coolness toward them in the pages of the early book on Forster. For Trilling, intellectuals live in terms of mind alone; and mind alone, fueled by will and conducting forever its researches into itself, is rarefied and treacherous. Intellect cannot understand the "strange virtue of weariness" or "the life of acceptant calm."

It is to that virtue and that life that Trilling's affections turn in *Sincerity and Authenticity*, most notably in his passage—almost a blissful interlude—on Jane Austen. She was concerned, he says, "for the defence of 'the honest soul,' with its definitive quality of single-mindedness and sincerity" (p. 72). She was not dialectical, but categorical. *Mansfield Park* even suggests that "Hegel is quite wrong" (p. 77), for that book tells us that nobility is to come only through affirmation, and not negation, as he believed. Baseness can lead only to baseness, as the example of Henry Crawford shows. Her noble characters, on the other hand, give the lie to Rameau's fragmented nephew. But in saying all this, Trilling really cannot bring himself to believe it. The satisfactions that Jane Austen can give are transitory and vulnerable. She is wholly antimodern, and hence pleasing, but that is not enough. She "comforts" us by recalling to our minds an archaic thought now banished from them: "things are what they really are, not in the unfolding future" (p. 80). But once her comfort has been absorbed and once her wonderful pleasures have been taken in, we return to ourselves; and those selves, as Trilling knows, are obliged to thrive on terrain untouched by Jane Austen. She can provide us with an unbroken idyllic sense of "the old visionary norm," but Trilling knows, and knows we know, that only a small part of our selves can respond to such a norm: "As householders, housekeepers, and parents we maintain allegiance to it in practice, possibly even in diffident principle. But as *readers*, as participants in the conscious, formulating part of our life in society, we incline to the antagonistic position" (p. 41).

One opposition keeping *Sincerity and Authenticity* alive as a book, then, and working implicitly to define its key terms, is that between "Austen" and "intellectuals." The first has to do with the categorical constraints of an older morality and an older psychology. The latter has to do with the painful divisions and impositions created by modernity. Trilling had always welcomed Austen into his world, giving her an extraordinary, almost improbable, stillness and pastoral appeal. And he had always resisted the full implications of the modern intellectual's presence, finding it fractious. Intellectuals make for a heightened awareness, an anxiety, and a sense of deep resentment in those they touch. They make the fundamental and necessary workings of society difficult. Austen represents the society that can and must function. Intellectuals represent a dysfunctional society. When, a few years after *Sincerity and Authenticity*, Trilling commented publicly that the "repudiation" of the middle class from itself is "all literature has been about for the last 200 years," or when he said that "art is one of the things that generated this consciousness" of disaffection, or when he then went on to denigrate both literature and education,[5] he was bringing to the surface some of the deeper strategies of this last book and he was summing up hostilities latent in his thought for decades.

The hostilities provide us with a way to speculate on the

style of mind present everywhere in his writings and most
elaborately so in *Sincerity and Authenticity*. How to explain
the deep modulations, self-reflexiveness, and high unambi-
tiousness of so many of its arguments? Geoffrey Hartman
once commented that Trilling "can read like a Commonplace Book, where thoughts remain *pensées*,"[6] and others
have observed that he writes without a sharp, predatory desire utterly to *convince* his readers, to bowl them over, to talk,
like Dr. Johnson, for victory. The explanation for this might
lie in his reluctance to become a cause of self-conscious divi-
siveness in others by employing a style divisive and fractious
itself. The modulations of his style conceal a hope about intellectual life at large. Antagonisms are to be attenuated
within and without.

Recognizing this, we can recognize something else: his
everlasting plea to welcome "complexity" and "variousness"
into all areas of intellectual life was but half-meant. Trilling
was, rightly enough, appalled by the rigidity of mind he saw
in others, but he had reasons of his own for guarding against
the full involvement of mind with idea, the full display of all
complexity and all variousness. There were tensions still best
kept closed, energies not yet to be encouraged, possibilities
to be kept submerged. Otherwise authenticity, thrust forward by intellect, would have its day and its chance to ruin.
Certain forms of repression were proper indeed.

Sincerity and Authenticity thus possesses an internal psychology of its own. The "honest soul" of the author, the
friend of "sincerity," is in perpetual conflict with the "base"
self associated with authenticity. The drama of the book consists of the ways in which the "base" self constantly gains
advantages over his "noble" counterpart. He badgers him
throughout the book. He is closer to all the better literature,
closer to Dostoevsky, to Conrad, to Nietzsche; he has stronger
affinities with Marx and Freud. Even history, as it declines
into modernity, appears to take up arms with him. Against
such stridency, the "honest" and "noble" soul can bring only

style, and insufficient style at that, made up of equivocations and reverence for a sensibility found in a largely symbolic Jane Austen and a historical moment prior to the origins of its relentless adversary. Even Trilling seems in very little doubt about the outcome of such a struggle.

The answer he proposes to the problem of having been placed at such a disadvantage is itself Hegelian. If the conflict between the "honest soul" and the "disintegrated consciousness" has in our time become overt, and if Hegel was right in prophesying the hegemony of the latter, the estranged critic like Trilling still might not be wholly without his power. He has at least the advantage of his estrangement. Hegel said that in some situations such an advantage would be sufficient to effect every needed change. Much of the latter half of *Sincerity and Authenticity* is therefore a confession of estrangement (there is "no self to be true to") and a simultaneous claim that to welcome estrangement might at last be to overcome it. Trilling's argument is thus as much therapeutic as it is exegetical. He wants to move through literature so that he may be able to move his self through it. Even when coping with his own marginality (and, by implication, the marginality of all those like him), he remains a moral critic. But he is forced also to become a self-correcting and self-healing critic. If we are all ill, as Freud announced, then no less are we all inauthentic, announces Trilling. And upon that inauthenticity must be imposed, he says, the authenticity derived from art. "The authentic work of art," he says, "instructs us in our inauthenticity and adjures us to overcome it" (p. 100).

His acceptance of estrangement and its uses involves his acceptance of Nietzsche and Oscar Wilde. His characteristically all-too-brief discussion of them turns entirely on their willingness not to be "selves" and to relinquish their illusions about identity. Wilde had said that "man is least himself when he talks in his own person. Give him a mask and he will tell you the truth." He had also said that "the truths of metaphysics are the truth of masks" (pp. 119–20). Nietzsche had said that "every profound spirit needs a mask" (p. 119). Declarations such as these seem to have genuine importance to Trilling because they give him license to surrender his "sincere" selfhood and submit to something more imperious. He had known for years that modernity would exact a tribute like that. To write, to be a critic, is always to wear a mask, to provide for oneself a consistency, or reliable authoritativeness, that obscures or resolves the conflicting "selves" that constitute a living sensibility. Not to concede that truth about the way we all contrive a being that shall meet the world is to remain in innocence. The tone of *Sincerity and Authenticity* is concessive; it is passive in the presence of things its author recognizes as having a strength greater than himself. "A real book reads us," he had long ago paraphrased Auden as saying; "some of these books at first rejected me; I bored them. But as I grew older and they knew me better, they came to have more sympathy with me and to understand my hidden meanings."[7]

The passivity of style in *Sincerity and Authenticity* issues, then, from the passivity its arguments promote. Mind and identity are to be at the disposal of something other than self; the idea is older than Keats, who called it "negative capability" and who believed it to be at least as old as Shakespeare. Trilling makes it a modern argument by giving as much dramatic coloration as possible to the beneficial onslaught of modernism. He tells his readers that the word "authenticity" comes from "*Authenteo*: to have full power over; also, to commit a murder," and he says that the modern has always had about it a murderous aura:

Sometimes we are a little puzzled to understand why this art was greeted upon its first appearance with so violent a resistance, forgetting how much violence there was in its creative will, how ruthless an act was required to assert autonomy in a culture schooled in duty and in obedience to peremptory and absolute law, and how extreme an exercise of personal will was needed to overcome the sentiment of non-being (pp. 131–32).

Trilling's moment of etymology is ingenious, wonderfully fortunate, and not a little specious.* But it allows him to stress the notion that one becomes modern by self-annihilation, and that modern art can be an accomplice in such annihilation. He thus wishes to vindicate modern art and the modern artist. They have done what their mere audience cannot do. They have retrieved sentiment of being, and have done so by employing will. Artists are hence privileged in ways the rest of us are not. They best know how to use will. We have not yet arrived at that privilege, and are wisest when most submissive in the face of art.

The estrangement we as mere readers experience is therefore one that can be sharply reinforced by the subtle authority of art. Art will not please, Trilling says, but it can provide the spiritual substance of life. This is not a religious argument, and to the higher religious reaches of experience Trilling's mind apparently never moved. None of his essays is a religious essay, and none of his assumptions or conclusions is religious. The argument here is a psychological one; it is concerned with emotional mastery. He says that ". . . the artist, even while he asserts his perfect autonomy and regards his audience with indifference, or with hostility and contempt . . . is sustained by the certitude that he alone can provide what the audience most deeply needs" (p. 98).

---

*If such violent meanings of "authenticity" are forgotten, and he says they are, then they are forgotten. Nor are they, as he says, "explicit in the Greek ancestry of the word" (p. 131). They are only implicit, and implicit but for a short time. Apparently by the first century A.D., the particular meanings of αὐθέντης as "an actual murderer, or self-murderer," had been lost. What was kept was the modern legacy of the verb αὐθεντέω, meaning "to have power over." It was this word that supplied the Greeks with αὐθεντικός, "of first-hand authority, original," the Romans with *authenticus*, and Old French with "autentique." The connotations Trilling would wish the word now to carry have been utterly absent for a long time, and his efforts to read them back in

On this reciprocal relationship Trilling establishes his credo as a critic. The audience needs its artist; the artist needs his audience. The two are to be kept separate, however, and their respective missions well defined. The responsiveness they have to each other constitutes the dialectical ordeal of modernity. Anything that closes the gap between artist and audience, anything that erodes the sharp differences within which the process of estrangement takes place, is illicit. That erosion can be known by another word: inauthenticity.

Trilling has been thought by some readers to be a reactionary in his attitudes toward modernism, to be no more than an aesthete maintaining the values of *belle-lettrisme.** This is erroneous. Trilling is devoted in *Sincerity and Authenticity* to the circumstances of modernism. His real fear is that, as circumstances, they will collapse. His hostility therefore goes out to the latter-day misunderstandings, or counterfeits, of modernism: "At the present moment, art cannot be said to make exigent demands upon the audience. The segment of our culture which is at all responsive to contemporary art is wholly permeable by it. The situation no longer obtains in which the experience of a contemporary work begins in

---

are an example of the defects of argument-by-etymology. Those arguments are usually corrupt because they can usually prove anything.

*See, for instance, Mark Krupnick, who believes that Trilling practices "an enervating overrefinement and preciosity . . . in which literary criticism is conceived as a kind of connoisseurship, involving acts of assessment no different fundamentally than in the case of Japanese swords or Greek and Chinese urns." Krupnick drinks deeply of the spring of the late 1960's and charges Trilling with "implicit snobbishness" and "mandarin exclusiveness" ("Lionel Trilling: Criticism and Illusion," in *Modern Occasions*, I, no. 2 [Winter 1971], p. 286). A stranger response to the challenges offered by Trilling was made by Roger Sale, who, thinking about Trilling's reputation in the 1970's, said both that reading him bears "certain affinities with eating a meal consisting entirely of Thousand Island dressing" *and* that, all things considered, "Trilling is assured and accurate when he retells the history of High Culture, and if such a history can show us the modern consciousness becoming born, Trilling can do the showing" (*The Hudson Review*, XXVI, no. 1 [Spring 1973], pp. 242–43). Sale really cannot determine what he feels about Trilling and ends his essay with perhaps the most substanceless charge of all: that Trilling "just does not write well enough."

resistance and proceeds by relatively slow stages to a comprehending or submissive admiration" (p. 98 n.). This, then, is
inauthenticity. Tensions lose their force, polarities dissolve.
The struggle of the modern, Trilling believes, must be kept
a struggle. In the 1950's he was worried lest the study of literature lose its complexity and thereby be eclipsed by the
growing complexity of politics. He said then that literature
must be given "an appropriate complication."[8] Now he is
anxious lest the generative tensions of modernism, a modernism he has learned to accept, should wholly slacken and die.
He says that we must repudiate "the unprecedented prolifera-
tion of art, the ease with which formerly esoteric or repellent
art-forms are accepted, the fascinating conjunction of popular and commercial art with what used to be called advanced
art." We must repudiate these things, understanding that we
do so because they "do not support the old belief that art
fosters a personal autonomy" (p. 67). As a cultural dialec-
tician, Trilling finds himself in a position in which he wants
his adversary to thrive, for only then may *he* thrive. Once
again he is John Stuart Mill asking that his adversaries be
truly formidable. As an intellectual sensibility, he wants the
conflicting aspects of his self—each of them—to be given full
manifestation. And as a psychological being confronted by
culture, he wants his deeper and authentic self, the disintegrative self, to enjoy its fullest sway.

His desires are, of course, Freudian in a traditional sense.
Trilling respects the old, "immitigable" Freudian arrangements, and his respect is expressed in Hegelian terms. He
wants to maintain differences between the internal life and
the external, between subject and object. He *wants* tensions
and reconciliations, estrangements and reversals. He *wants*
the crises of spiritual death and rebirth. The Freudian drama
possesses many of the same elements as the Hegelian; M. H.
Abrams has described the latter as "the unwitting quest of
the spirit to redeem itself by repossessing its own lost and
sundered self, in an ultimate recognition of its own identity

whereby, as Hegel says . . . , it can be 'at home with itself in its otherness' "[9] For Trilling, modern culture, preserved with its authenticity intact, provides the only arena in which such crises can occur. He might at times wish to avert his gaze from it, and to find solace within a quieter landscape, but the liveliest pages of *Sincerity and Authenticity* demonstrate that he knows that he should not and cannot do so. The drama he thus enacts in the pages of his book is also Freudian. In his alternations between acceptance and rejection of modernity, between tolerating its demands and wishing release from them, he is, to quote his own words, "an organism in which the ceaseless effort to survive is matched in strength by the will to find peace in extinction" (p. 155). Those alternations have informed and defined his career as a critic. However much he has addressed himself to the prospects of death— and to the finalities and transcendence it would provide in a world of conflict, error, and triviality—so much, too, has he addressed himself to the fertile complexities of life as literary culture gives them force.

In bringing Freud to his support as he enacts this struggle, Trilling pursues the oldest notion he has had as a critic: that the conditions of life are not really negotiable. The complexities evoked by literature are involved with conditions and tensions whose foundations are unalterable. Freud's attention, particularly in his career's later stages, was centered, as Trilling's has been, on the "immitigable." *Sincerity and Authenticity* ends, however, as Trilling turns his surprised attention to the possibility that this primary assumption might be wrong. He knows that strong intellectual authority, deeply aware of Freud but opposed to the noble grandeur of Freudian pessimism, has lately questioned the assumption. He also knows that the questioning has focused on the terrible primacy enjoyed in psychological life by the superego.

Trilling's history of the discovery of the superego by Freud and its subsequent prominence in discussions of the tragic limitations of mankind is dense, almost cryptic. The Oedipal struggle, he says, has had as one of its effects the creation of a part of the unconscious responsible for the faculties of moral judgment and self-criticism. Yet this aspect of the unconscious is something more than conscience, and behaves in ways that reveal its functions as belonging to more than mere conscience. Those functions have become autonomous, responsive neither to ego nor to society. Once a part of ego, those functions have now made ego their permanent victim. The punishment the superego inflicts upon the ego Freud called guilt; this guilt, originating in the Oedipal tangle, is never to be lifted. The cruelty of the superego therefore consists in the fact that though it "demands renunciation on the part of the ego, every renunciation which the ego makes at its behest, so far from appeasing it, actually increases its severity" (p. 153). The ego, as a sort of executive authority, suppresses the antagonisms against the father issuing from the id; yet the very aggressions suppressed by the ego are employed by the superego to intensify its dominance over the ego. The process, as Trilling describes it, is unrelenting. He sums up his exceedingly brief explication by saying: "It will be enough if we understand that although it was to serve the needs of civilization that the superego was installed in its disciplinary office, its actual behavior was not dictated by those needs; the movement of the superego from rational pragmatic authority to gratuitous cruel tyranny was wholly autonomous" (p. 154).

Trilling's account is, thus far, faithfully responsive to the Freud of *Civilization and Its Discontents*. Trilling recognizes, where Freud had recognized before, the pain of being alive in society. No change is to come to this spectacle, for it is rooted in biology, in the nature of being human. Social forms are only the superstructure established on this fixed design. Trilling is not willing, however, to let the merely immutable alone. He wants to bestow on Freud a deeper basis for his skepticism, a firmer set of reasons for his "dark doctrine." In sum, he is not satisfied that Freudian logic alone is now persuasive enough to guarantee Freud's wisdom, his

supremacy in our time as a thinker and a prophet, his invulnerability to attack and criticism from those who have of late
questioned the "immitigability" of life.

In a word, Trilling is not satisfied with the mere "truth" of
Freud. This he admits, saying he wants more than truth—
namely the *will* beneath the doctrine, the "authenticity" beneath Freudian "sincerity." For Trilling, as we have seen,
had never been much interested in some of Freud's technical
or clinical formulations, particularly as they involved the
explicitly sexual, the infantile, the specific dynamics of the
unconscious, and the world of dreams. His attention had been
riveted for years on Freud's metaphyschological and prophetic
force, not on how the small, intricate steps of his argument
were to end at last in proof. Trilling believes that Freud had
ulterior motives for doing what he did. These motives were
in the highest of causes. They had, says Trilling, "the intention of sustaining the authenticity of human existence that
formerly had been ratified by God. It was his purpose to keep
all things from becoming 'weightless' " (p. 156).

Once we understand how Trilling thus steps over Freudian
reason and Freudian machinery on the way to Freudian authority, we can better understand the closing pages of *Sincerity and Authenticity*. They mean to convince not by logic,
but by thrusting against the latter-day opponents of Freud
the charge that they are inauthentic, that they have made less
of life by permitting it to be seen as insubstantial and manip-
ulable.

Chief among these opponents are Norman O. Brown and
Herbert Marcuse. Trilling recognizes them both as schooled
in Freud, and hence formidable in ways that people ignorant
of Freud are not. He had as early as 1959 said of Brown's *Life
Against Death* and Marcuse's *Eros and Civilization* that they
had made "a contribution to moral—and, by implication,
political—thought which cannot be overestimated." [10] They
were opposed to the simple-minded optimism of neo-Freu-
dians such as Erich Fromm and Karen Horney. They had, in

addition, passed another of Trilling's tests: they had rejected
the kind of psychoanalysis "blandly conceived by the progressive wing of the American middle class. . . ."[11] So far, so
good, at least for Trilling. Brown and Marcuse had confronted what was bitter in Freud. Brown in particular was
praised by Trilling for "the complexity he is willing to ascribe
to the etiology of the human illness, and the inherent difficulty of cure that he implies even as he says that a cure must
be found or we perish."[12]

All of this had seemed welcome to Trilling in 1959. And
Brown's thesis even seemed plausible then. Perhaps there was
something meritorious in a challenge to Freud that was
mounted on wholly secure Freudian grounds. If one could
accept repression, tragedy, and death—if one could accept the
superego and all that its formation implied about life—and
then go on to controvert the stern prophecies growing out of
their acceptance and to supplant them with other prophecies,
then one's bravery was remarkable. "What I have called Mr.
Brown's courage lies in his acceptance of the grounds for the
Freudian pessimism," Trilling wrote, "and *then* challenging
the pessimism."[13]

A decade before *Sincerity and Authenticity* he saw that
challenge arising, explicitly from Brown and implicitly from
Marcuse, as a plea that human beings recover their "erotic exuberance," their physical bodies, and their joyful narcissism.
Then the ravages of the superego would be stopped. The
sublimations and repressions on which the superego feeds
would be lifted. By lessening the aggressive energies allied
with death, and by redirecting them, we would: ". . . cease
to strengthen and pervert the death-instinct, which, in its
strengthened and perverted form, manifests itself in the dominance over our minds of the category of time, in fear, in rigorousness, in aggression, in repression, in sterility."[14]

Everything we know about Lionel Trilling as a writer contributes to our understanding of him as a man who carried

with him thoughts of mortality. He fixed his attention on death because he recognized how sharply it framed the issues of life. It judged, and could be seen daily to judge, the limits and capacities of every human enterprise. To ignore it, in literature, in politics, in society, was to ignore the very force that itself never ignored any living thing. For Trilling, then, the notion that somehow the terrible truth of death could be eased by a reformulation of human activity and understanding was immensely important.

In 1970, he sees that extraordinary notion rising up not just to contravene Freud, but to provide a wholly new understanding of life itself. It had become, he saw, a new gospel of the times and was in the hands of a thinker who had become a prophet of that new generation at odds with Trilling's own. Marcuse, the most secular and optimistic of the "Frankfurt School," spoke for some part of the "adversary culture," and he did so with force because, as I have said, he had absorbed the lessons of Freud only to go beyond them. Could Marcuse, then, represent for Trilling a new and more devastating authenticity to which all previous authenticities must stand as secondary? Was the authenticity for which Freud and Trilling had argued now to be seen as only a disguised bit of sincerity? Was the connection to death not as necessary, as ineluctable, as they had thought it to be?

Trilling centers his attention on Marcuse's treatment of the superego. In *Eros and Civilization* Marcuse declares that technological advances have simply diminished, in our time, the force of material necessity and economic constraint in our lives. We are now free enough to imagine an existence in which the harsh and gratuitous monitoring of the superego will become vestigial and, at last, utterly feeble. The circle of coercion, renunciation, and guilt will be broken. The death-instinct itself, rooted in the superego, will be drained of the energy of its aggression against the self. Hence the hypocrisy, or bad faith, involved in traditional Freudian dichotomies and tensions will no longer be relevant, and a floodgate of previously pent-up energies will emerge in their true form—the polymorphously perverse.

To this fine and glorious utopian prospect Trilling makes no direct or detailed response. He does not, that is, argue with it by engaging with the terms and strategies set forth by Marcuse. He establishes his own terms of response, and those he employs with his customary rhetorical skill. His strategy is simply to tell Marcuse that the evolution of consciousness described in *Eros and Civilization* is one that will erode human character. Without the tensions and constraints previously so dense a part of life, human existence will indeed possess polymorphous perversity. But it will not possess hardness and toughness. It will not possess texture, nor "weight." Trilling shrewdly points out to Marcuse that this state of reduced individuality will be, moreover, the breeding ground of a new and terrible political totalitarianism. More than shrewdly, Trilling wisely reminds Marcuse that he, Marcuse himself, a product of nineteenth-century ethical rigorousness, ". . . *likes* people to have 'character,' cost what it may in frustration" (p. 166).

As far as Trilling is concerned, this is answer enough to Marcuse and all he represents. Trilling believes he has refuted him in a compelling, even devastating, way. He has come upon a contradiction not to be resolved. Marcuse, even a Marcuse armed with revolutionary fervor, cannot create a vision more authentic than the one to which Trilling, and Freud, have remained faithful. Marcuse's authenticity is no authenticity at all, but a vision totally abstracted from life. The grounds on which Trilling makes this judgment do not issue, as I say, from argumentation. They issue from *will*, from rooted conviction. Just as Trilling wanted more than reason and argument from Freud, and wanted to see the *will* beneath the Freudian doctrine, so here he tries to secure his advantage over Marcuse by noting that, whatever Marcuse's arguments embody, they do not uphold *character*. And the will, on Trilling's part, for people to have character is the high cause he has served all his life. It is a cause sustained by literature; it is not to be subordinated to anything else. It is what Arnold and Forster, Rousseau and Diderot, James and Wharton, Conrad and Joyce had taught him. After all is said and done, it is the thing he knows best.

On this note the book ends, but not until Trilling pleasurably annihilates the contemporary idea that in an "insane" society only the insane are truly sane. Insanity does not, he declares, possess any such commanding authenticity. The insanity endorsed by the psychiatrists David Cooper and R. D. Laing, their "antinomian reversal of all accepted values, of all received realities" (p. 171), is not to be credited at all. Insanity is not even an adequate response to the circumstances of life, much less a successful renunciation of them. When Cooper and Laing argue the merits, therefore, of "an upward psychopathic mobility to the point of divinity, each one of us a Christ" (pp. 171–72), they are blind to the circumstances through which the historical Jesus made his painful and much-obstructed way. He had, as a small part of his larger inconveniences, to reason with rabbis and make sermons. His "mobility" was of the uncertain and wayward sort, moreover, with which literature has always been concerned. It is, in fact, Cooper and Laing who have, in Trilling's eyes, the truly unencumbered motion, for they may ascend wherever their ideas take them. They, and not their hapless patients, have the "freedom" of madness. The historical Jesus, and all great and substantial literary characters, and Freud, and Trilling himself, are heavily encumbered. Environment, history, and a clutter of details encroach upon them always. Beneath all this clutter, but never in ignorance of it, they would secure their authentic selves. The obscure and hazardous process by which they attempt to do so is the subject of literature. The literature most powerful in tracing the process is a central subject of *Sincerity and Authenticity*. The history that literature has taken in the last 400 years provides the structure of the book.

Trilling's arguments are, in this crucial sense, conservative. But to be charged with having been conservative in such a manner, and for so long, would have been a characterization he more than gladly would have welcomed. To have arrived only where he began—with a devotion to literary understanding as the means by which the authenticity of experience could be defined and judged—may be seen, after all, as a disappointment, but a very high disappointment indeed. *Sincerity and Authenticity* "fails" to move beyond literature. Much as it stands in awe of the fully realized literary act, and much as it resists the imposing authority of literary modernism, it comes ultimately to stand equably in the presence of modernism. In its pages, Trilling reasons with many rabbis, and his sermons are numerous. He often "undertakes to intercede," and he indicates at last that by 1970 he had known the peculiar pleasures "of beginning something and at a certain point remarking that it is finished" (p. 172). His capacity as a critic may be measured by the attention he paid, and the anxious fidelity he offered, to one particular creation of the human mind—literature—he knew he could never subordinate. Neither to a system, nor to a conception of society and politics, nor to his own private wish that passivity and resignation end the tumult of the day would the energies of literature submit. In knowing that truth, Trilling judged correctly the strength of his familiar adversary.

years, aspired to social and political ideals but did so with an innocence about historical circumstances and social complexities.* They floated toward abstractions, leaving behind them the bitterness and difficulty of actual situations. They wished to ignore the cost that human individualism has to pay on the way to becoming human socialization. They tended to be a "weightless" people circulating aimlessly within a "weightless" culture. But who, specifically, those people were was not a disclosure either Trilling's argument or his rhetoric was inclined to provide. His polemical stances made him turn not to particular targets, but to general ones. Rahv and Hook, Kazin and Macdonald, Howe and the others just named were not the "weightless" people he apparently had in mind. Hardly so, and hardly guilty had they been so charged. Who, then, was being charged? Trilling never said, and his prose style reflected a tactical graciousness that disallowed the internecine attack. He wrote to criticize "tendencies"; and when on rare occasions he did mention individuals, such as V. L. Parrington or R. D. Laing, they mattered only as unprepossessing examples, drawn from afar, either in time or geography. Of greater matter was Trilling's way of complimenting his readers by implying that they were not "weightless" and that they certainly would not fall victim to the debilities suffered by the likes of Parrington or Laing.

As Arnold's student, Trilling patiently struggled for his whole career to renew the belief that the value of literature rests on its "weight," its evocation of the human, its reminder of specifically human dimensions, its understanding of human

---

*An attitude about the 1930's shared by his wife, the critic Diana Trilling, but expressed by her in characteristically more polemical and bitter terms. That time, she has written, ". . . far from being the most moral decade of this century, the quickest and most irradiated with right feeling, was almost entirely built upon self-deception and the deception of others. . . . [In] consequence it left a legacy of debilitating ignorance." Review of Samuel Hynes, *The Auden Generation*, in the *New York Times Book Review* (May 22, 1977), p. 40. See also her essay "Liberal Anti-Communism Revisited" in *We Must March My Darlings: A Critical Decade* (New York, 1977), pp. 41–66. She there refers to the 1930's as making "the great intellectual rift in this country" (p. 45.).

desire hemmed in by human failure. And if literature is to have any value at all to Americans, that value must be seen as rising out of literature's opposition to a characteristic direction of American mind and sensibility. Literature would lead its readers, its American readers, back to their moral selves, to the "sentiment of their moral being," the very place many of them were reluctant to go.

As we know, this Arnoldian faith in literature was submitted in Trilling's lifetime to the harshness of another lesson. The high truculence of modern literature had demonstrated that literary culture might provide only flimsy support at best to moral awareness. Modern literature had become divisive and sullen and in other quarters merely playful and whimsical. Céline and Burroughs were one sort of disturbing modernism, the "camp" sensibility another. Trilling can be thought of as at home with neither. And so, with increasing discomfort, he came to ask: For what good reason should modern literary culture be encouraged? In the extract just given, Trilling reminds the editor of *Commentary* magazine, Norman Podhoretz, who had been his student at Columbia and had now become a member of a later generation of American intellectuals, that his ambivalence about literature is "old." So it is. Trilling had grown wary much earlier about art: it could indeed weaken. "Genius" should not always be greeted with open arms, for it could be destructive. He had long been anxious about the uses of the intellect: it might grow too powerful and unleash a turbulence that could sap cultural stability. Was not education, allied with literature, intellect, and will, suspect for the same reasons?

Between these two attitudes, the faithful and the suspicious, Trilling's mind found its place as his career came to an end. *Sincerity and Authenticity* illustrates the pain his loyalty to literary culture had come to entail. To be at ease with that culture, particularly as it sought to determine for itself an autonomy at odds with middle-class beliefs, had become more difficult for him. As a reader of Freud, he knew that his problem was part of something larger—the unease that *any* individual has to endure in being involved in *any* culture. The torpid urbanity of his later style, its involutions and recessiveness, reflected his hesitancies in the face of something he saw growing more imperious than himself. Occasionally, as in his lecture and pamphlet of 1972, *Mind in the Modern World*, he sought to project his own difficulties onto aspects of the culture itself. In that pamphlet, he speaks resentfully of an ". . . ideological trend which rejects and seeks to discredit the very concept of mind."[2] He neglects, however, to note the extent to which his own writings had never wholly credited mind, and had always shared in an attitude he now chooses to reprehend, namely, the "resentment of the authority of mind."[3]

Part of the story of Lionel Trilling's substantial and paradoxical importance to his fellow intellectuals, and to American intellectual history, is the manner, then, in which he reserved the gravest doubts about intellectual life. As a literary critic, he never really wished intellectual life to gain complete authority over the social life of which it was just one part. Intellect itself was rootless and maverick, just as Edmund Burke had long ago said; hence it should be limited and defined, colored and modulated, by other forces. One might say that the "little platoons" of particular experience, and of mundane reality, should act to impede the monolithic working of mind.* "Genius" should never run free; it should al-

---

*Critics entranced by the freest workings of mind and the fullest expansions of consciousness are habitually troubled by Trilling. No matter how much they admire his slow elegance of expression, they are reluctant to respect as much as he the social "stuff" in which his gravity is rooted. Thus Denis Donoghue, comparing Trilling with R. P. Blackmur, says "Trilling's mind distrusted the temptation to aspire beyond the finite condition to a state of being that is absolute, unconditioned, peremptory, detached from public consequence." For Donoghue, as for Blackmur, this distrust is not wholly admirable, for to both of them consciousness has an imperiousness not to be denied save at the cost of subtracting from art and from intellectual life their finest energies. I argue that Trilling saw some of those energies as destructive and was willing to pay the cost. See Denis Donoghue, "Trilling, Mind, and Society," *The Sewanee Review*, LXXXVI, no. 2 (Spring 1978), p. 166.

ways be made to encounter the interference of social reality. The reason for Trilling's doubts about mind, and for his considerable importance nonetheless in the community of intellectuals of his time, rests on the fact that he possessed a uniquely compelling literary sensibility. It was a sensibility that recoiled from the incursions of modernity, but that nevertheless affirmed the literary comprehension of reality. Literature opened his mind to complexity and to the conditioned character of mental existence. At the same time, it made him see that pure mental life is a phantasm. Thinking exists in life, but should never find absolute sway over it.

That other thinkers of his time could assent to Trilling's reservations about intellectuality is important in several ways. That they agreed in spirit with him is, first, an indication of the inherent persuasiveness of his position. Second, such agreement is an indication of the deference they felt still appropriate to literature and to the literary model of experience. As social scientists, political theorists, or historians, they could regard themselves as "humanists" while in Trilling's authorial presence. A younger writer, Roger Sale, hostile to Trilling but aware of his importance, has accurately said of him that he was the only critic read by such people, and that by virtue of their reading and endorsements he "was widely known in American universities."[4] Part of Trilling's fame rested on the way he gave general treatment to morality and politics and thereby extended himself beyond the traditional confines of an English Department. He was attentive to history and responsive to context, thus welcoming to his thought disciplines other than his own. His repudiation of the ahistorical and apolitical thrust of the New Criticism was his way of affirming, early in his career, the relevance of matters beyond the textual.* But it was also a way of saying that the technical

---

*Robert Langbaum, one of Trilling's admirers, cites Trilling speaking at the University of Virginia shortly before his death: "He got on to the subject of structuralism; and concluded by saying that thirty years ago he had fought against Stalinism and that he would, if he were young, fight structuralism

narrowness into which any intellectual pursuit, even the practice of literary criticism, can fall should be broken open by
the wholeness of human response that literature alone seems
able to give. That is one function of imagination, and Trilling wanted to be able to praise imagination all his life. Uncomfortable as he grew older in being able to do so, he nonetheless never wished a New Criticism (although who the New
Critics exactly were, he never, in his typical fashion, made
clear) to descend on any of the mind's pursuits.

In speaking of him as "our teacher," Steven Marcus, a long-
time Columbia colleague and a critic deeply influenced by
Trilling's example, says that "it is extremely uncommon to
find someone who actually believes in the real world—whatever that may be—and who believes further that literature
has some determinate and important relation to that world."
Trilling was for Marcus and many others uncommon in just
that way, continuing "to assert that society really exists."[5] And
Marcus is certainly right in recognizing that assertion on
Trilling's part, even though he does not draw attention to
Trilling's other side, that contrary impulse on his part to give
even social circumstances themselves an abstract quality, a
cerebral and airy presence. Nonetheless, Trilling's faith in
the real existence of society—a tough fabric in which history,
political event, and economic situation are interwoven with
the artist's peculiar aspiration—made him a literary critic accessible to a multitude of nonliterary thinkers. Daniel Bell,
Richard Hofstadter, David Riesman, Philip Rieff, C. Wright
Mills, Daniel P. Moynihan, Irving Kristol, Seymour Martin
Lipset, and Richard Sennett have all had occasion, as have
had many others, to employ Trilling's ideas or expand upon
them. The respect and adulation Trilling received from such

---

today as another system antithetical to will and individual freedom." See "The
Importance of *The Liberal Imagination*," *Salmagundi*, 41 (Spring 1978), p. 65.
Trilling, like many American critics of his age and background, saw struc-
turalism as no more than the New Criticism revisited, but *à la française*.

thinkers, particularly in the last decades of his life, amounted to tacit agreement with him about the appropriate limits of pure thought. His Burkean conservatism on the matter of un-obstructed cerebration was also theirs.

In sum, Trilling had convincingly elaborated a means to return discussions of literary works to the cultural roots and the social circumstances from which they had arisen. The so-cial scientists and theoreticians involved in the study of such conditions welcomed a literary thinker who believed in the substantiality of the real world. But Trilling's belief in that world extracted from him a cost in his critical power. The world of society is a world of prose. It can be quite uncom-fortable with poetry. And Trilling was never at home, as a critic, with poetry. He wrote about poets like Wordsworth and Keats, about their moral dimensions, but he did not write with ease about the inner life of their poetry. Uncomfortable not only with poetry but also with the kind of literature originating in a repudiation of social circumstances and his-tory, he was, in essence, not happy with art liberated from its constraints and filiations. The novel, particularly the nineteenth-century novel, could best acknowledge those con-straints. In wanting writers to make that acknowledgment, Trilling wanted critics and readers to make it also. Yet he saw that everywhere around him it was not being made. Marcus is correct in observing that Trilling was not wholly free of the Platonic wish to banish poets from the ideal society. Nor was he at odds with Rousseau's notion, cited in *Sincerity and Au-thenticity*, that ". . . literature . . . is the pre-eminent agent of man's corruption, the essence or paradigm of the inherent falsehood of civilized society."[6] The makers of literature, hav-ing become powerful in their artistic mastery, were now judged by him to be irresponsible since they would not sub-mit to the demands of the world as it must, for the greater good, really be. Trilling would not and could not banish such writers. But he would grow wary in the presence of the eva-

sions, fantasies, and nihilistic impulses that he believed much
modern literature had ingeniously cultivated. Art, he thought,
was not at its best when it nourished the destructive elements,
nor best when it was mere symbolic action such as that created
by Samuel Beckett, whom he never learned to like. It was at
its best as a form of moral action, as action leading to other
action. A consequence itself, it was good when it had morally
enriching consequences. But, intrusive and dangerous as it
was, modern literature could not be left alone. Trilling knew
it was the literature that the past, and modern circumstances,
had given us. It too was a consequence, and dislike it though
he might, he could not deny it. There *was* something formidable and "exigent" about Kafka, Lawrence, Beckett, Joyce,
and Proust. There was no use in ignoring such genius and
pretending the literature of benignity alone existed.

But when Trilling was able to turn his attention away from
modernity, and to think about literature in general, he saw
it as an integument. It covered history and covered society,
uniting itself with them. In so doing, moreover, it allowed
itself to be covered; and a literature that did not evoke the
causes out of which it had come was, for Trilling, no real
literature at all. In 1970, when he presented to a general reading audience his views on the growth of literary criticism, he
observed that it, too, was "consequential." Criticism was, as a
human achievement, one way of observing how society was
continually engaged in answering the challenges that literature had placed before it. "That literature should have called
into being an attendant art of judgment [criticism] tells us
something about the nature of literature—that it is an enterprise which is inherently competitive,"[7] he wrote in an introduction to a collection of classic literary criticism. He also remarked there on the rich density of relationship that must
properly, even if painfully, be maintained between the public
power of the author and the intimate privacy of the reader.
He knew that the reader competes with the writer, that each

"reads" the other. The writer's work invades the reader's sensibility and demands from him a response:

> What is the legitimacy of the power over us that Shakespeare exercises through *King Lear*? He overcomes our minds, requiring us to behold things from which we want to turn away in horror and disgust. . . . By what right does he do this? By what right does any author invade our privacy, establish his rule over our emotions, demand of us that we give heed to what he has to say, which may be wholly at odds with what we want to hear said if we are to be comfortable?[8]

Trilling was, after much anxiety, convinced that most of this kind of competitiveness in the past had been proper and that the energies consumed in almost all of its challenges had been well spent.

But times had changed. The "adversary culture" had escaped from such a train of consequence, and, in time and with much brilliance allied to it, had reintroduced itself to the world of consequence, of action, of readership and criticism. It had risen above, and then had come to denigrate, the world of intellectual understanding, tacit agreement, and cultural consensus. The middle class, which had given to the "adversary culture" its writers, and then its audience, had become in time the central object of its hostility. The result was, Trilling thought, ugly: internecine warfare within the largest and most important social class of modern Western history. As he looked on—just as Matthew Arnold before him had looked on—at that spectacle, he believed, and he sought to make his readers believe, that a deterioration of that class's best sense of itself was now fully under way.* Its self-esteem

---

*In 1973, Trilling's close friend and Columbia colleague Jacques Barzun expressed sentiments remarkably similar in spirit. In *The Use and Abuse of Art* (*The A. W. Mellon Lectures in The Fine Arts*), Barzun sees the modern artist as "having left behind sweetness and light" and as now participating in "the liquidation of 500 years of civilization." This destruction involves, for Barzun, a nightmare vision of "misuses and misunderstandings—*Macbeth* boiled down to 80 minutes, *Wuthering Heights* or *Tom Jones* on film, Leonardo on T.V., Rabelais staged in a few scenes, Shakespeare in the Park, humanities programs for the hinterland, sunrise semester for the culture-hungry

had been eroded, its strengths checked. The disintegrative process had begun with French and German Romanticism, with the rise of the *avant-garde*, with the Marxist tradition developing in the long aftermath of the French Revolution. The turmoil of the 1960's was just the latest stage. With local evidence to hand such as the temporary radicalization of the Modern Language Association and the affirmative action edicts of the U.S. Department of Health, Education, and Welfare, Trilling writes in *Mind in the Modern World* that there had been ". . . within the intellectual life of the nation, and not of our nation alone, a notable retraction of spirit, a falling off in mind's vital confidence in itself."[9] Perhaps "mind" in time will revitalize itself and assert its presence in our national culture, but Trilling in this essay seems very doubtful.

His disenchantment was a long time in the making. That is why, even with evidence so ephemeral as that in *Mind in the Modern World*, he comes in 1972 to fear ". . . a diminution of national possibility . . . a lessening of the social hope."[10] His local evidence is not important; his foreboding is. It is rooted in his long-standing belief that the drama of attaining some form of selfhood, of individual autonomy, is the central drama of life, the process to which all other processes pay heed. Selfhood is pursued, moreover, *against* the grain of experience which culture provides. The process is nothing if not adversarial. It assumes an external and an internal set of forces. In their struggle, each of those forces aspires to mastery. Culture will have its way. But so indeed will the singularity of the individual. Culture, in its fullness and richness, will exact from the individual the cost, in domestication, of his pursuing a civilized life. And the individual will continue to

---

before breakfast, digests and anthologies and all-you-need-to-know-about-art-in-one-handy-volume. . . ." All is crassness, vulgarity, fragmentation, and volatile disorder. See *The Use and Abuse of Art* (Princeton, N.J., 1974), pp. 137, 141, 146.

resist making that payment, claiming it to be an intolerable submission. Almost all of the literature Trilling was interested in, and liked, reflected that conflict. The outcome of the struggle could be, at best, a *rapprochement*, a stillness, a moment of art, which could temporarily act to hold in suspension the tumult and anxiety of the struggle. Such moments could make the situation tolerable. Trilling praised them when they had become artistic form.

It was clear to him, however, that the advantage in the conflict had in the modern period shifted massively in favor of the external force, that of society and socialization. The possibilities of an autonomous selfhood, held gracefully in opposition to everything else in the serenity of artistic achievement, had been almost entirely lost. The artistic experience was, like everything else, in the process of being devoured by society. Art of all kinds, even the most intimate and the most painful, had become popular and commercial. Such art, and the moments of profound individuality it mirrored, were now absorbed, just as everything else was absorbed, by the nature of modern cultural experience. Clement Greenberg and Dwight Macdonald had now been proved wrong: "kitsch" had not eclipsed "elite" art. Rather, "elite" art had everywhere taken over, and had become its own kitsch.

Irving Howe says that Trilling, in his last years, was seeking ". . . an art of sensual candor and carefree transparency which would not repudiate the entanglements of modernism but would rest at ease with, or against, them."[11] Everything we know about Trilling's career makes us recognize both the appropriateness of that search, and its futility for him. He had always wanted to find a way of entering into equilibrium with the ravages of modernity. But he could never believe that the act of criticism could arrive at that equilibrium. Why? Because criticism, no matter how decorously accomplished, is by definition an adversarial undertaking. It is the pawn of will and intellect, of energy and desire. It, too, lacks serenity.

Art alone, and only the very best of art, possesses serenity.

Jane Austen, for instance, now occupies a station in our culture that will remain permanently distant from the power of modernism to neutralize everything in its path. In an essay written in the last year of his life, and in part concerned with Austen, Trilling observed: "However committed to expressive action and significant utterance the Western paradigm of personhood may be, the Western person, as I have suggested, is not wholly without the capability of finding value in what is fixed, moveless, and silent."[12] In Jane Austen's work, that value of the "moveless" and "silent" inheres, or so Trilling says. He then moves on in the essay to make a general observation about a problem central to his career as a writer. He discusses the power of death to symbolize the power of art, and says that with Hamlet, Macbeth, or Lear, ". . . the process of destiny must come to a stop: a point is reached at which each hero ceases to be a manifestation of will and comes to exist for us as idea or representation, as an object completed and, as it were, perfected."[13] Part of our gratification as readers issues, then, from our toleration of the beneficence of death. We know it has a peculiarly intimate relationship to the perfections of art. We accept the complicated process by which will is ". . . transmuted into an object of representation, carried by appropriate death beyond the reach of contingency."[14]

If we, like Trilling, wish to move beyond contingency in all its injurious aspects, and if we are determined to see that some art can attain the security of being noncontingent, then it is not difficult to understand the kinship of art and death. They are allied in the real world because they are allied in our minds. Trilling says that the human spirit contains: ". . . the perception that art, even when it is at pains to create the appearance of intense and vigorous action, has the effect of transmuting that which is alive into that which has the movelessness and permanence of things past, assimilating it in some part to death."[15]

Once again, and now as the culmination of a discussion

with himself about death, a discussion he had pursued for years, Trilling sees how best he might understand, and put to use, the finality of death.* In his early stories, he had recognized death as a means of moral judgment. To understand death was directly to understand self and, in the case of "The Other Margaret," to see, as William Hazlitt had once seen, what separated youthful dreams from wise maturity. In *The Middle of the Journey*, death had political meaning. It could be used to judge the vacuities of progressive idealism and middle-class liberalism. It must be accepted, just as E. M. Forster had accepted it, as a presence continual in our lives. And if we are to understand ". . . this strange disease of modern life," we must come to terms with Freud's magisterial sense of death. To do so will give us further understanding of that moment in Trilling's career when he comes to his powerful apprehension of James Joyce, who represents to him a nihilism of splendid dimensions. Death was for Joyce, as it was for Trilling, one great reality, perhaps the greatest. They would both have concurred with George Santayana that "everything that man does between birth and death is an effort to escape the one overpowering fact, that we must all die." There is, however, no morbidity in that recognition. Indeed, Trilling and Joyce based their wholly different writings on the absolute importance of first comprehending the "everything" that man does, not the nothing toward which his actions inevitably lead. Neither thought very highly of those who could not, or who on principle would not, look to the specific circumstances and gritty particularities of a given life. It was there, down there, that literature, and criticism, must begin.

*We may note the coincidental aspects of the respective careers of Trilling and Freud. Writing in 1961 on Freud, Trilling says: "As he grows older, he is conscious of great fatigue, he speaks often of diminished energies and he is more and more occupied by the thought of death. . . ." Trilling mentions also ". . . that one relationship which many men of advancing years find it difficult and often impossible to sustain—his relationship with himself." "Introduction" to Ernest Jones, *The Life and Work of Sigmund Freud*, ed. and abridged by Lionel Trilling and Steven Marcus (New York, 1961), p. xii.

To argue for so long about death and its useful truths, and for so long about life and its best exemplifications, and to do so with a sustained, if not untroubled, trust in literature as a criticism of life, was to be much more than a literary critic. Lionel Trilling has been judged a moralist, or a historian of moral consciousness, or a philosopher of culture. None of these designations does him perfect justice, but they are just in one particular respect: it is not the specific findings of his literary writings, the isolated remarks and *aperçus*, that give him his unmistakable value to the culture in which he lived. His many thoughts and reflections must not, in fairness to him and to other critics whose methods obviously differ from his, be considered *thought* in any pure sense. He was not a theorist and he left to the future no coherent philosophy of literature. Nor was his writing left undamaged by his vague critical terms, by their portentousness and blurred immensity. Nor, it may selfishly be said, did he write *enough*. Joseph Frank has asked why he did not write a book on Jane Austen and has said that it is a pity that "so much of his later writing was occasional and (usually) obliquely polemical."[16] Other readers will have wanted other things; but the books that might have been are the essays that are.

Rather than historian, philosopher, or theorist, Lionel Trilling was a sensibility who patiently cultivated thinking in order to subsume it to the rhythms of his search for wisdom. His worth, and his rare distinction, will outlive his individual essays. And his identity as a critic will, in time, be disentangled from the provinciality of his milieu. He is more than the narrow term "New York critic" can suggest. Like Edmund Wilson, he will be seen as a writer who sought always to rise above the conventions and shibboleths of his immediate surroundings. Both Trilling and Wilson, the two most important American literary critics of the mid-century, refused to let the art of criticism rest in the confines of academic specialization. Wilson, a decade Trilling's senior, represents a broader and more various achievement; his curiosity was greater, his learning more far-ranging. But Trilling went more deeply than did Wilson into the problems he took as his own. This difference noted, another similarity should be mentioned: both saw how attractive, and yet how delusory, organized political behavior could be.

Wilson surveyed more from his vantage point of dispossessed old-fashioned American cantankerousness and probity than did Trilling from his position as deracinated, aloof, and inquiring university teacher. But Trilling pursued more energetically than did Wilson the ways in which he could employ the terms of literary criticism to understand the struggle for self-knowledge his reading evoked in him. He will be seen in the future as a critic who, by examining certain aspects of literature, helped to enlarge his readers' sense of moral complexity. For that good and valuable reason, he will, I believe, outlive in importance other critics now deemed more fashionable. He reminds us all, and has reminded me for many months in writing this book about him, of something we can never wholly forget: literature is important by virtue not of its textuality but of its entry into our moral lives. That is an "old-fashioned" truth; Trilling, like Wilson, was old-fashioned.

Literature was, in Trilling's apprehension of it, the criticism of life in being the criticism of a life. That life, his own, never averted its attention from two extraordinary realities: the power of death and the corruption of doctrinaire politics. He was both eschatological and of his time and place. He judged present conditions, and the art and persons such conditions had placed in prominence, in the light afforded by the inevitability of death and the distinctly unforgettable barbarisms of Stalin. In being such a judge, Trilling worked always to define the mutable self within him, to recognize its enormous complexities and contrary imperatives. By his example, he helped to make more clear the same struggle of definition and recognition in his readers. His self demonstrated, in his prose, its affinities with those other selves. Literary criticism is a quiet, always imperfect, collective enterprise. It unites critic and reader. It was sustained, for years, by the drama of Trilling's self-critical examinations. His excellence is found in that drama.

Notes

Notes

Preface
1. Jacques Barzun, "Remembering Lionel Trilling," *Encounter*, XLVII, no. 3 (Sept. 1976), p. 82. Stendhal's epitaph in Montmartre reads "Arrigo Beyle, Milanese, Scrisse, Amò, Visse" (he wrote, he loved, he lived).

Chapter 1
1. Irving Howe, "On Lionel Trilling," *The New Republic*, 174, no. 11 (Mar. 13, 1976), p. 30.
2. Lionel Trilling, "Preface" to *Beyond Culture* (New York, 1968), p. xii.
3. Trilling, *Beyond Culture*, p. 8.
4. Trilling, "Preface" to *The Opposing Self* (New York, 1955), p. xi.
5. Trilling, "The Morality of Inertia," in *A Gathering of Fugitives* (Boston, 1956), p. 31.
6. Delmore Schwartz, "The Duchess' Red Shoes," in *Selected Essays of Delmore Schwartz*, ed. Donald A. Dike and David H. Zucker (Chicago, 1970), p. 212. Originally published in *Partisan Review*, XX, no. 1 (Jan. 1953), pp. 55–73.

Chapter 2
1. Lionel Trilling, "Young in the Thirties," *Commentary*, 41, no. 5 (May 1966), p. 43.
2. *Ibid.*, pp. 47–48.
3. *Ibid.*, p. 49.
4. Dwight Macdonald, "Introduction: Politics Past," in *Memoirs of a Revolutionist* (New York, 1958), p. 15.
5. Irving Howe, "The New York Intellectuals: A Chronicle and a Critique," *Commentary*, 46, no. 4 (Oct. 1968), p. 40.
6. Trilling, contribution to "Under Forty: A Symposium on American Literature and the Younger Generation of American Jews," *Contemporary Jewish Record*, VI, no. 1 (Feb. 1944), p. 16.
7. Trilling, "Young in the Thirties," p. 47.
8. *Ibid.*
9. As quoted in Alan M. Wald, "The Menorah Group Moves Left," *Jewish Social Studies*, XXXVIII, nos. 3–4 (Summer-Fall 1976), p. 294.

10. Trilling, "Young in the Thirties," p. 49.

11. Howe, "The New York Intellectuals," p. 32.

12. William Phillips, "What Happened in the 30's," in *A Sense of the Present* (New York, n.d.), p. 23.

13. David A. Hollinger, "Ethnic Diversity, Cosmopolitanism and the Emergence of the American Liberal Intelligentsia," *American Quarterly*, XXVII, no. 2 (May 1975), p. 140.

14. Trilling, "The Function of the Little Magazine," in *The Liberal Imagination: Essays on Literature and Society* (New York, 1953), p. 96.

Chapter 3

1. Lionel Trilling, "Impediments," *The Menorah Journal*, XI, no. 3 (June 1925), pp. 286–90.

2. Trilling, "The Changing Myth of the Jew," *Commentary*, 66, no. 2 (Aug. 1978), p. 34. This essay was written in 1929, was accepted for publication in 1931 by *The Menorah Journal*, but never appeared there. Its appearance in *Commentary* came, that is, almost fifty years after it was written.

3. Trilling, "Why We Read Jane Austen," *Times Literary Supplement* (Mar. 5, 1976), p. 252.

4. Trilling, "Chapter for a Fashionable Jewish Novel," *The Menorah Journal*, XII, no. 3 (June–July 1926), pp. 275–82.

5. Trilling, "Funeral at the Club, with Lunch," *The Menorah Journal*, XIII, no. 4 (Aug. 1927), pp. 380–90.

6. Trilling, "A Light to the Nations," *The Menorah Journal*, XVI, no. 4 (Apr. 1928), pp. 402–8.

7. Mark Van Doren, "Jewish Students I Have Known," *The Menorah Journal*, XIII, no. 3 (June 1927), pp. 267–68.

8. Trilling, "Of This Time, of That Place," *Partisan Review*, X, no. 1 (Jan.–Feb. 1943), pp. 72–81.

9. Trilling, "Commentary" included with reprinting of "Of This Time, of That Place" in *The Experience of Literature: Fiction* (New York, 1967), p. 359.

10. *Ibid.*, p. 360.

11. *Ibid.*

12. Trilling, "The Other Margaret," *Partisan Review*, XII, no. 4 (Fall 1945), pp. 481–501.

Chapter 4

1. Arthur Schlesinger, Jr., as quoted on the cover of the Avon Library paperback edition (1966); Daniel Patrick Moynihan, "An Address to the Entering Class at Harvard College, 1972," *Commentary*, 54, no. 6 (Dec. 1972), p. 58.

2. Trilling, "On *The Middle of the Journey*," *The New York Review of Books*, XXII, no. 6 (Apr. 17, 1975), p. 23. This doubled as the Introduction to the reissue of the novel in 1975.

3. *Ibid.*, p. 20.

4. *Ibid.*, p. 19.

5. William James, *The Varieties of Religious Experience* (New York, 1930), p. 100.

6. Sigmund Freud, "Thoughts for the Times on War and Death," *Collected Papers*, vol. 4 (London, 1953), p. 316.

7. Philippe Ariès, *Western Attitudes Toward Death: From the Middle Ages to the Present* (Baltimore, Md., 1974), p. 87.

8. Robert Warshow, "The Legacy of the Thirties: Middle-Class Mass Culture and the Intellectuals' Problem," *Commentary*, 4, no. 6 (Dec. 1947), p. 544. Reprinted, with some revisions, in Warshow, *The Immediate Experience: Movies, Comics, Theatre, and Other Aspects of Popular Culture* (Garden City, N.Y., 1962), p. 47.

9. Irving Howe, "On *The Middle of the Journey*," *The New York Times Book Review* (Aug. 22, 1976), p. 31.

Chapter 5

1. Robert Warshow, "The Legacy of the Thirties," in *The Immediate Experience*, p. 47 (see full cite in chap. 4, n. 8, above).

2. *Ibid.*, pp. 37–38.

3. *Ibid.*, pp. 48, 39.

4. Lionel Trilling, "Edmund Wilson: A Backward Glance," in *A Gathering of Fugitives* (Boston, 1956), pp. 50–51.

5. Trilling, *Matthew Arnold* (New York, 1955), p. 336. The book was first published in 1939.

6. Matthew Arnold, "Irish Catholicism and British Liberalism," from *Essays Religious and Mixed*, ed. R. H. Super (Ann Arbor, Mich., 1972), p. 346.

7. Trilling, "The Situation in American Writing: A Symposium," *Partisan Review*, VI, no. 5 (Fall 1939), p. 111.

8. Philip Rahv, "Proletarian Literature: An Autopsy," in *Literature and the Sixth Sense* (Boston, 1969), p. 14. Originally published in *The Southern Review*, IV, no. 3 (Winter 1939), pp. 616–28.

9. Trilling, "The Situation in American Writing," p. 109.

10. Trilling, "Introduction" to George Orwell, *Homage to Catalonia* (Boston, 1955), p. xiv. Reprinted as "George Orwell and the Politics of Truth" in Trilling, *The Opposing Self* (New York, 1955), p. 162.

11. Karl Marx and Frederick Engels, "Manifesto of the Communist Party," in Karl Marx and Frederick Engels, *Selected Works* (Moscow, 1968), p. 44.

12. Trilling, "The Function of the Little Magazine," in *The Liberal Imagination* (Garden City, N.Y., 1953), p. 92. Originally published, in slightly different form, as the "Introduction" to *The Partisan Reader: Ten Years of Partisan Review, 1934–1944: An Anthology*, ed. William Phillips and Philip Rahv (New York, 1946).

13. Trilling, "Introduction" to *The Portable Matthew Arnold* (New York, 1949), p. 7.

14. *Ibid.*, p. 8.

15. As quoted in Trilling, *Matthew Arnold*, p. 172.

16. Trilling, "Introduction" to *The Portable Matthew Arnold*, pp. 8–9.

17. Trilling, "The Novel Alive or Dead," in *A Gathering of Fugitives*, pp. 125–32.

18. Clement Greenberg, "Avant-Garde and Kitsch," in *Art and Culture: Critical Essays* (Boston, 1961), p. 10.

19. *Ibid.*, p. 8.

20. Trilling, *Matthew Arnold*, p: 349.

21. *Ibid.*, p. 208.

22. *Ibid.*, p. 209.

23. John Henry Raleigh, *Matthew Arnold and American Culture* (Berkeley, Calif., 1957), p. 231.

24. Trilling, *Matthew Arnold*, p. 231.

25. *Ibid.*, p. 232.

26. *Ibid.*, p. 233.

27. Raleigh, p. 232.

28. Trilling, *Matthew Arnold*, p. 352.

29. *Ibid.*, p. 353.

Chapter 6

1. Matthew Arnold, *Culture and Anarchy*, ed. J. Dover Wilson (Cambridge, Eng., 1957), p. 108.

2. Lionel Trilling, "The State of American Writing, 1948: A Symposium," *Partisan Review*, XV, no. 8 (Aug. 1948), pp. 888–89.

3. *Ibid.*, pp. 892–93.

4. Edmund Burke, *Reflections on the Revolution in France* (New York, 1961), p. 19.

5. Trilling, "The Situation of the American Intellectual at the Present Time," in *A Gathering of Fugitives* (Boston, 1956), p. 68. Originally published as Trilling's contribution to "Our Country and Our Culture, A Symposium," *Partisan Review*, XIX, no. 3 (May 1952), pp. 318–26.

6. Stephen Spender, "Beyond Liberalism," *Commentary*, X, no. 2 (Aug. 1950), p. 190.

7. *Ibid.*, p. 192.

8. Trilling, "Editor's Note," *The Portable Matthew Arnold* (New York, 1949), p. 433.

9. Trilling, "Treason in the Modern World," *Nation*, 166 (Jan. 10, 1948), p. 46.

10. Trilling, "Elements That Are Wanted," *Partisan Review*, VII, no. 5 (Sept.–Oct. 1940), p. 372.

11. John Henry Raleigh, *Matthew Arnold and American Culture* (Berkeley, Calif., 1957), p. 224.

12. John Stuart Mill, "Coleridge," *Essays on Ethics, Religion and Society*, ed. J. M. Robson [*Collected Works of John Stuart Mill*, Vol. 10], (Toronto, 1969), p. 163.

13. Trilling, *E. M. Forster* (New York, 1964), p. 58. The book was published originally in 1943.

14. Trilling, *Matthew Arnold* (New York, 1955), p. 182.

15. Trilling, "Preface" to *The Liberal Imagination* (Gardon City N.Y., 1953), p. vii.

16. *Ibid.*

17. Trilling, "The Situation in American Writing: A Symposium," *Partisan Review*, VI, no. 5 (Fall 1939), p. 110.

18. Trilling, *E. M. Forster*, pp. 3–4.

19. *Ibid.*, pp. 138–39.

20. *Ibid.*, pp. 63–64.

21. *Ibid.*, pp. 13–14.

22. *Ibid.*, p. 22.

23. *Ibid.*

24. *Ibid.*, p. 173.

25. *Ibid.*, p. 181.

26. *Ibid.*, p. 122.

27. *Ibid.*, p. 123.

28. *Ibid.*, p. 124.

29. *Ibid.*, p. 125.

30. Trilling, "Elements That Are Wanted," p. 374.

31. Raleigh, p. 225.

32. Trilling, "Elements That Are Wanted," p. 375.

33. *Ibid.*, p. 376.

34. Trilling, *E. M. Forster*, p. 184.

Chapter 7

1. David Caute, *The Fellow-Travellers, A Postscript to the Enlightenment* (London, 1973), p. 275.

2. Harold Rosenberg, "The Cold War," in *Discovering the Present: Three Decades in Art, Culture and Politics* (Chicago, 1973), p. 303. Originally published in *Partisan Review*, XXIX, no. 1 (Winter 1962), p. 76.

3. Lionel Trilling, *E. M. Forster* (Norfolk, Conn., 1964), p. 184.

4. Sigmund Freud, *Civilization and Its Discontents*, ed. James Strachey (New York, 1961), p. 62.

5. Stephen Spender, "Beyond Liberalism," *Commentary*, 10, no. 2 (Aug. 1950), p. 191.

6. R. W. B. Lewis, "Lionel Trilling and the New Stoicism," *The Hudson Review*, 3, no. 2 (Summer 1950), p. 317.

Chapter 8

1. Lionel Trilling, "The Situation of the American Intellectual at the Present Time," in *A Gathering of Fugitives* (Boston, 1956), p. 65. Originally published in *Partisan Review*, XIX, no. 3 (May 1952).

2. *Ibid.*, p. 66.

3. *Ibid.*
4. *Ibid.*
5. *Ibid.*, p. 72.
6. Trilling, "Art and Neurosis," in *The Liberal Imagination: Essays on Literature and Society* (New York, 1953), p. 174.
7. William Arrowsmith, "All About Ripeness," *The Hudson Review*, 8, no. 3 (Autumn 1955), p. 447.
8. T. S. Eliot, "The Metaphysical Poets," in *Selected Essays* (New York, 1960), p. 247.
9. Denis Donoghue, "The Critic in Reaction," *Twentieth Century*, 158, no. 944 (Oct. 1955), p. 379.

Chapter 9

1. Robert Lowell, "The New York Intellectual," *Notebook 1967–68* (New York, 1969), p. 112.
2. Robert Mazzocco, "Beyond Criticism," *The New York Review of Books*, V, no. 9 (Dec. 9, 1965), p. 23.
3. Mazzocco, p. 22.
4. Lionel Trilling, "James Joyce in His Letters," *Commentary*, 45, no. 2 (Feb. 1968), p. 53. The quotation is from *The Letters of James Joyce, Volume III*, ed. Richard Ellmann (New York, 1966), p. 359. The original Italian reads "Adesso termino. Ho gli occhi stanchi. Da più di mezzo secolo scrutano nel nulla dove hanno trovato un bellissimo niente."
5. Trilling, "James Joyce in His Letters," p. 57.
6. *Ibid.*, p. 54.
7. *Ibid.*, p. 55.
8. *Ibid.*, p. 53.
9. *Ibid.*, p. 64.
10. *Ibid.*

Chapter 10

1. As Donald Davie put it: "We see here one of the most distinguished minds of our time 'at the end of its tether,' questioning the assumptions on which it has proceeded through an admirably responsive lifetime, and coming up with no sure answers." *Manchester Guardian Weekly*, 108 (Dec. 30, 1972), p. 22. Trilling's career was spent, as we have seen, in wariness of those who had fashioned sure answers to cultural problems. Interestingly enough, Trilling refers to H. G. Wells's *Mind at the End of Its Tether* on the opening page of *Mind in the Modern World* (1972).
2. Stephen Donadio, "Columbia: Seven Interviews," *Partisan Review*, XXXV, no. 3 (Summer 1968), pp. 386–87. Others interviewed were Immanuel Wallerstein, Peter Gay, Eric Bentley, Mark Rudd and Lewis Cole, Ray Brown and Bill Sales, and Charles Parsons.
3. William Butler Yeats, as quoted in Richard Ellmann, *Yeats: The Man and the Masks* (New York, n.d.), p. 278. The original source for

the statement is an unpublished note among MSS of the first edition of Yeats's *A Vision*.

4. Richard Poirier, *The Performing Self: Compositions and Decompositions in the Languages of Contemporary Life* (New York, 1971), p. xiii.

5. "Culture and the Present Moment: A Round-Table Discussion," *Commentary*, 58, no. 6 (Dec. 1974), pp. 46–47. Trilling goes on in this conversation (p. 48) to add that "in a certain sense I am arguing against education."

6. Geoffrey H. Hartman, review of *Sincerity and Authenticity, The New York Times Book Review*, Feb. 4, 1973, p. 28.

7. Trilling, *Beyond Culture: Essays on Literature and Learning* (New York, 1968), p. 8.

8. Trilling, *The Liberal Imagination: Essays on Literature and Society* (Garden City, N.Y., 1953), p. 183.

9. M. H. Abrams, *Natural Supernaturalism: Tradition and Revolution in Romantic Literature* (New York, 1971), p. 230.

10. Trilling, "Paradise Reached For," *Mid-Century Review* (Fall 1959), p. 17.

11. *Ibid.*, p. 18.

12. *Ibid.*, p. 19.

13. *Ibid.*, p. 20.

14. *Ibid.*, p. 21.

Chapter 11

1. Lionel Trilling, contributions to "Culture and the Present Moment: A Round-Table Discussion," *Commentary*, 58, no. 6 (Dec. 1974), pp. 39–40, 46, 48.

2. Trilling, *Mind in the Modern World: The 1972 Jefferson Lecture in the Humanities* (New York, 1972), p. 30.

3. *Ibid.*, p. 31.

4. Roger Sale, "Lionel Trilling," *The Hudson Review*, XXVI, no. 1 (Spring 1973), p. 241.

5. Steven Marcus, "Lionel Trilling, 1905–1975," *The New York Times Book Review* (Feb. 8, 1976), pp. 34, 32. Reprinted in Quentin Anderson, Stephen Donadio, and Steven Marcus, eds., *Art, Politics, and Will: Essays in Honor of Lionel Trilling* (New York, 1977), pp. 265–78.

6. Trilling, *Sincerity and Authenticity* (Cambridge, Mass., 1972), p. 60.

7. Trilling, *Literary Criticism: An Introductory Reader* (New York, 1970), p. 1.

8. *Ibid.*, p. 4.

9. Trilling, *Mind in the Modern World*, p. 41.

10. *Ibid.*

11. Irving Howe, "Lionel Trilling: A World of Remembrance," *Salmagundi*, 35 (Fall, 1976), p. 3.

12. Trilling, "Why We Read Jane Austen," *Times Literary Supplement* (Mar. 5, 1976), p. 252.

13. *Ibid.*

14. *Ibid.*

15. *Ibid.*

16. Joseph Frank, "Appendix (January 1978)" to "Lionel Trilling and the Conservative Imagination" (1956), *Salmagundi*, no. 41 (Spring 1978), p. 53.

Index

Index